The White House

An Illustrated History

*Part of the Presidential Seal is carved into the front
of the president's desk in the Oval Office.*

The painting on the previous page, Fourth of July at the White House,
by Patricia Palermino was a gift to President and Mrs. Ronald Reagan.

The White
House
An Illustrated History

CATHERINE O'NEILL GRACE

SCHOLASTIC NONFICTION

Published in cooperation with the
White House Historical Association

A portion of the proceeds from the sale of this book will be directed to the educational programs of the White House Historical Association, a nonprofit organization.

Library of Congress Cataloging-in-Publication Data ★ Grace, Catherine O'Neill, 1950– ★ The White House: An Illustrated History/by Catherine O'Neill Grace. ★ p. cm. ★ Summary: Explores the history, architecture, and symbolism of the White House, which serves as a museum, office, ceremonial site, and a home to presidents and their families. Includes bibliographical references. ★ ISBN 0-439-42971-4 ★ 1. White House (Washington, D.C.)—Juvenile literature. 2. White House (Washington, D.C.)—Guidebooks—Juvenile literature. 3. Washington (D.C.)—Buildings, structures, etc.—Juvenile literature. 4. Presidents—United States—Juvenile literature. [1. White House (Washington, D.C.) 2. Washington (D.C.)—Buildings, structures, etc. 3. Presidents.] I. Title. ★ F204.W5 G723 2003 ★ 975.3—dc21 ★ 2002030603

10 9 8 7 6 5 4 3 2 1   03 04 05 06 07

Art direction: Nancy Sabato ★ Book design by Jaime Boyle / Red Herring Design

Printed in the U.S.A.   23   First printing, October 2003

★   ★   ★   ★   ★   ★   ★   ★   ★

This fire screen kept the heat off President Ulysses S. Grant's guests to the White House.

For Don Grace, whose abiding love for
American history helps me understand my country

Acknowledgments

Any book is a collaborative venture, this one more so than most. I would like to thank, first of all, the staff at the White House Historical Association, particularly John P. Riley, director of education and scholarship programs. Hats off to you, John. Thanks also to the WHHA's director of publications, Marcia Mallet Anderson; historian Bill Bushong; photo archivist Harmony Haskins; and photo researcher Katie Marages. My thanks to the many wonderful people I met at the White House itself, especially Claire A. Faulkner, from the Usher's Office, who made it possible—and comfortable—for me to spend time in our nation's most important home. I much appreciated curator William G. Allman's informative tour and curator emeritus Betty C. Monkman's careful review of the manuscript. I am grateful to the men and women profiled in the "Faces & Voices" section of this book for so generously sharing their time and memories with me. Thanks to Martha Davidson for photo research and to Maggie Knaus for sensitive original photography. At Scholastic, editorial assistant Danielle Denega tirelessly tracked thousands of photographs and art director Nancy Sabato guided the book's gorgeous look and feel. I was also lucky enough to have the guidance of a gifted Scholastic editor, Kate Waters. Finally, I would like to acknowledge the remarkable role the White House itself played in this project. Its presence and power are unrivalled. I have walked past it since I was a little girl, and it has never lost its magic. Getting to know it better only increased my respect and gratitude. Can one thank a building?

I guess I just did.

—Catherine O'Neill Grace

Sand Dunes at Sunset, Atlantic City, *by Henry Ossawa Tanner, is the first painting by an African-American artist in the White House Collection. It was a gift of the White House Historical Association.*

Foreword

Thomas Jefferson trained his secretary, Meriwether Lewis, to take a dangerous journey of discovery. British troops burned our nation's capital city. The first man on the moon made a phone call to the Oval Office. A Middle East peace treaty was signed. A war on terrorism was planned. All these events have one thing in common—they all happened at the White House. As the office of the president of the United States, the White House has been the site where many of the most important acts and difficult decisions in our history have been made.

The White House Historical Association (the Association) tells those stories of the White House because it is important for young people to know what it has been like for presidents, first ladies, and their families to live in this structure, which is not only a home and an office, but also a museum. In 1961, with the help of First Lady Jacqueline Kennedy, the Association began its work to create books, films, and classroom materials about the building first known as the President's House. Leaders and their families come and go in our democracy, but the house and what it stands for stays the same.

One reason the White House seems unchanging is that the Association helps preserve it and the historic objects it houses. A group of experts works with the first lady to decide how to decorate the house and to select its paintings, furniture, and china. The Association also helps purchase selected objects that are related to the house and its first families so that people can enjoy them when they visit.

There is no place like the White House. It is a living historic house. Each day, the president, his family and his staff use it. People, both young and old, visit it. The White House holds the echoes of President Abraham Lincoln and President John F. Kennedy, yet it is ready to serve President George W. Bush. We hope this book will inform and inspire you as you see how the White House reflects the past, the present, and the future of the United States.

Work in progress. White House rooms are kept fresh for the first family and visitors. The White House Historical Association funded a Red Room renovation in 2000.

Neil W. Horstman

President, White House Historical Association

U.S. Marines guard the doors of the West Wing lobby when the president is in the Oval Office.

Contents

Dear Readers

Reach out and read. Mrs. Laura Bush, a former librarian, enjoys reading to children. She has made a campaign for literacy part of her efforts as first lady.

As a young girl growing up in Texas, I never imagined that one day I would live in the White House. This historic building is more than 200 years old and has stood as America's home since 1800. From John Adams to George W. Bush, the White House has served as an office and a home for every American president and his family.

The president and I enjoy living in the White House. We have family dinners here, read books, and watch television just as you do in your home. We also play with our pets—our cat, Willie, and our two dogs, Spot and Barney. The White House is larger than any doghouse Spot and Barney have ever seen. There are 132 rooms, 35 bathrooms, and 12 chimneys.

The White House is a very exciting place to be. Many interesting people come to work here every day. You will get to know some of them as you read this book. For photographers and gardeners, policy makers and writers, carpenters and chefs— the White House is an office.

The White House is also a museum, and thousands of visitors come here to experience America's history. Here, President Abraham Lincoln signed the Emancipation Proclamation; and President Franklin D. Roosevelt delivered his famous radio addresses, called "fireside chats." The White House has many beautiful paintings and pieces of historic furniture. President Bush uses the same desk that nearly every president in the past 120 years has used.

There is a great deal to do and discover in the White House. As you read this book and learn more about this historic home, remember that the White House is your home, too. As the president says, the White House is the "People's House." I hope that you will visit the White House, and that some day you may even have the opportunity to work or live in America's home.

Laura Bush

A Symbol of FREEDOM

People all over the world recognize the name "the White House." Those three simple words call up an image of a centuries-old white, rectangular mansion in downtown Washington, D.C., surrounded by a vibrant modern city. An American flag flies proudly from its roof.

This house, which from its beginning has been a family home as well as the office of the president of the United States, has been a stage for American history since John Adams moved here in 1800. Here presidents have celebrated victories. Here they have signed laws that change lives. Here they have planned wars and wept over losses. Here presidents who have died in office have been mourned by their families and by the nation.

The White House is a house. But it is also a symbol of the United States. It stands for freedom and democracy. It is a beacon for people in other countries who turn to the United States for help. As a symbol of freedom and hope, it is one of the most important buildings in the world.

The White House is also a symbol of free speech. Visitors sometimes see protesters making their opinions known in front of its gates. These protesters show that in the United States it is safe and legal to peacefully disagree with the government and to express opinions freely.

The White House is also a symbol of our democratic elections. It reminds people that after elections our government changes hands peacefully. On Inauguration Day the outgoing president greets the incoming president at the door of the White House, welcoming him to his new home. The White House belongs to our government, so it belongs to each of us. It is our house.

Please come inside!

Welcome to Washington! Children holding Mexican and American flags line up on the White House South Lawn to welcome Mexico's President Vicente Fox as he visits President George W. Bush.

FACES & VOICES

Gary Walters, Chief Usher

Important buildings like the White House are inspiring to look at and exciting to visit. But without the people who work within them, they are not much more than bricks and mortar, carpeting and curtains, marble and glass. In this book we will meet some of the people who make the White House run smoothly for the first family, who take care of the building and its treasures, and who communicate about it to curious children from all over the United States. As you read, watch for pages titled "Faces & Voices." You will meet some very interesting people!

To begin, we will meet Gary Walters, chief usher of the White House. If you walked in the front door of the White House, from the North Portico, his office would be the first room on the right side of the Entrance Hall. White House ushers have used this room as their office since the nineteenth century.

The pattern that is the background of all of the Faces & Voices interviews is from a quilt made from fabrics used on the furniture in the East Room, Red Room, and Green Room from 1897 to 1901.

Ready to go. Chief Usher Gary Walters stands in the Blue Room, which has been set up for a dinner. Mr. Walters keeps a sharp eye on all the details that make White House hospitality so special.

"My title, Chief Usher, comes from the past," Mr. Walters explains. "We greet people and usher them on to where they're going within the White House. Until 1902, the presidential offices were upstairs in the main building, so the usher actually showed visitors up to see the president. Now it's a combination term that also means head of the household."

Mr. Walters has worked at the White House since 1970. "It's an interesting place to be every day," he says. He began as a Secret Service officer, then joined the Usher's Office in 1976. He was named Chief Usher during President Ronald Reagan's administration and has worked for every president since, whether Republican or Democrat.

"This is a home and the president and his family have to be comfortable in their home," he says. Mr. Walters manages the household staff of 95 people—curators, housekeepers, maintenance people, carpenters, electricians, operating engineers, chefs, and butlers—who maintain the 132-room residence and take care of the president's needs. (The White House grounds crews, who take care of the gardens, work for the National Park Service.)

If Mr. Walters could show you around the White House, he says he would enjoy taking you to see the places where kids can play—the bowling alley, the movie theater, and the Children's Garden

created in the Lyndon Johnson administration. The busiest time in Mr. Walters's job comes when a new president moves into the White House.

"One family is moved out and another family moved in, in the time it takes to have the inaugural parade," he says. "Our aim is when the new president comes in from the inaugural reviewing stand, he feels at home. His clothes are hung in his closet; the first lady's shoes are where they're supposed to be; their favorite snacks are stocked in the pantry. We want them to know that this is their home, not a place they're visiting. We're here to make them comfortable."

Making an entrance. British Prime Minister Tony Blair and President George W. Bush enter the Cross Hall from the East Room as Chief Usher Gary Walters works in the background.

One Building,

When you look at the White House, you see a building, of course—an impressive and historic building. But the White House is more than simply a structure made of stone, brick, and steel. Much more.

For the first family—the president, first lady, and their children—the White House is an important symbol of our nation. But it is also their family home. In that home they do all the things that ordinary families do—play games, read, do homework, talk, watch TV, have parties, eat pizza, celebrate birthdays, and so on. But they do these ordinary things in an extraordinary space where past presidents and their wives and children have lived before them. When Laura Bush plays with her dog Barney on the South Lawn, she is playing where little Caroline Kennedy rode her pony. When President George W. Bush walks to the Oval Office in the morning, he is traveling the same route followed by his father, the forty-first president. When the first family gathers in the family quarters upstairs, they are in a place where Abraham, Mary, Willie, and Tad Lincoln also sat during their happy first days in the White House.

History is everywhere in the White House. It is in the rooms in which important events took place, such as the signing of the Emancipation Proclamation. History is in the objects that have been collected and treasured by past presidents. It is in the china, the artwork, and the furniture. The White House contains our history. It is a museum of our national heritage. Its objects and its stories belong to all of us.

White House walkways. First Lady Jacqueline Kennedy takes her infant son John for a stroll on a winter day.

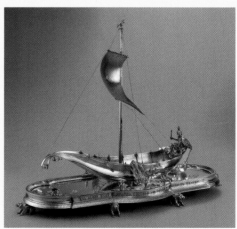

All alone went Hiawatha. This silver centerpiece, known as the "Hiawatha Boat," was selected in 1876 by Mrs. Julia Grant for the White House.

ROOMS
with a

In 1790, Congress voted to build and furnish a house for the president in the newly created capital city. President George Washington selected a building site on a high ridge overlooking the Potomac River. The land dropped from the ridge to marshes along the riverbank, providing a breathtaking vista of the glittering water in the distance. The White House stands on this ridge of land today.

Four Functions

The White House is also a working office for one of the busiest executives in the world, the president of the United States. In fact, it has been called the Executive Mansion, because the president is the chief executive, or leader, of the government. Presidents once worked upstairs on the second floor of the White House. Today the president uses the Oval Office in the West Wing as a place to read reports, meet with his staff and important visitors, think, talk to advisors, and make decisions that affect the lives of people all over the world. His Cabinet—a group of advisors who head government departments—and staff meet here as well. The White House is a busy place where historic things happen. There is no such thing as a slow day at the office when you work at the White House!

Pomp and circumstance. The Marine Band marches past to honor a visiting head of state, part of a welcoming ceremony on the South Lawn during the administration of President Richard Nixon.

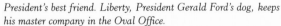

President's best friend. Liberty, President Gerald Ford's dog, keeps his master company in the Oval Office.

The president serves as the chief diplomat of the United States, the official who is in charge of maintaining friendly relations with other nations all over the world. Therefore, the White House is also a ceremonial site, the stage on which dramatic meetings between world leaders take place. Here Winston Churchill visited Franklin D. Roosevelt during the darkest days of World War II. Here the Israeli prime minister and Palestinian chairman met. Ceremonies and cultural events happen at the White House all year long.

VIEW

Building the President's House

From a distance. This 19th-century view of Washington shows the White House on the left perched upon a ridge. The Capitol is the domed building on the right.

Many monuments, roads, and fences have been erected around the White House since President George Washington stood on the hillside.

George Washington never lived in the house. He retired from office before it was finished. Instead, he and his wife resided in a redbrick house in Philadelphia. But as the government prepared to move from Philadelphia to the District of Columbia, Washington was deeply involved in planning and building a structure that would serve every president for years to come. The planners, architects, and American citizens called this house the President's House.

Thomas Jefferson was the secretary of state at the time. He drew up rules for a contest to design the house. The building would be important not only as the president's home and office, but also as the first public building in the new city that would be the permanent headquarters of the nation's government. In July 1792, Washington considered all of the plans that had been submitted and decided to give the job to James Hoban, an Irish-born architect who had been working in South Carolina. Hoban's design was a dignified mansion of stone. Its rectangular shape would make it easy to add additional wings to it in the future as the country and its government grew. Almost as soon as he had accepted it, Washington asked Hoban to change his design, adding more carved decoration and making the house bigger. But the finished house was actually smaller than originally planned. The young United States government did not have enough funds for a gigantic mansion.

In the fall of 1792, a crowd gathered on the ridge as a special stone called the cornerstone was placed in the foundation. George Washington was not there. A brass plaque attached to the cornerstone read:

> THE FIRST STONE OF THE PRESIDENT'S HOUSE WAS LAID THE THIRTEENTH DAY OF OCTOBER, 1792, AND IN THE SEVENTEENTH YEAR OF THE INDEPENDENCE OF THE UNITED STATES OF AMERICA.

The President's House was underway. The outer stone walls that Washington watched being built are still standing in the city that is named for him.

By 1794, the essentials of the structure we know today—including its oval reception rooms—had begun to take shape. Washington favored oval rooms, perhaps because he liked to greet his important guests as they stood in a circle around him.

A home in Philadelphia. George Washington lived in this red-brick house with his wife, Martha, when he was president. He was the only president who never lived in the White House.

BUILDING THE FIRST WHITE HOUSE

WASHINGTON D.C. 1798

An artist imagined the construction of the President's House under the watchful eye of George Washington.

In the Early Days:
The 18th Century

Architect and builder James Hoban faced a firm deadline for finishing the President's House. It was supposed to be ready for its first occupant by November 1, 1800. The construction work went on almost continuously for eight years.

There were many challenges to building a large house in the raw new city. Sandstone was readily available from a quarry on Aquia Creek, forty miles down the Potomac River in Virginia. But the blocks had to be delivered by ships and hauled to the building site. It was a slow process. (Experience taught that this stone cracked easily unless it was sealed. The builders solved the problem by whitewashing the sandstone, creating a white house.) Finding skilled workmen to carve

Scottish stonemasons carved beautiful designs seen here above the North Entrance.

decorations on the stone was difficult. A master stonemason from Scotland was hired, and from 1794 to 1798 about a dozen Scottish masons were busy at the site carving beautiful details for the exterior of the house. Black workmen, enslaved and free, also worked at the site. The many bricks needed to build the interior walls of the mansion could be made right there. The framing for the roof finally went up in 1797, the last year of Washington's presidency. The great hero of the Revolutionary War stopped by the unfinished building on his trip from Philadelphia to his Virginia home. Soldiers in the Washington Artillery were there to greet the general and president. They fired a sixteen-gun salute. It was the only official ceremony that George Washington ever attended at the President's House—the house that he had dreamed about and planned for so long.

After Washington left office and John Adams became president, progress on the President's House slowed as workers rushed to finish other public buildings in the city, such as the Capitol. It was 1800—the first year of a new century—when the state rooms of the President's House were wallpapered in anticipation of President Adams's arrival in the capital city. The president had been asking how the new house was coming along. He was worried that there was no vegetable garden, so one was quickly planted before he arrived.

On November 1, 1800, Adams moved into the unfinished house. His wife, Abigail, joined him two weeks later. Only half of the 36 rooms were plastered. Only one of three planned staircases had been built—the winding back stairs that went from the basement to the upper floors. Adams spent his first afternoon in the President's House greeting callers. Then he had supper, took a single candle, and climbed the dark, winding staircase to the second floor to go to bed.

The next day, in a letter to his wife, President Adams wrote these words:

"I pray Heaven to bestow the best of blessings on this house and on all that shall hereafter inhabit it. May none but honest and wise men ever rule under this roof."

Today, you can see these words carved into the mantelpiece in the State Dining Room.

Changes and Challenges: The 19th Century

John Adams and his wife, Abigail, lived in the White House only a few months because he was defeated in the presidential election of 1800. Mrs. Adams may have been pleased to move out. She found the house damp and chilly. "The great unfinished audience room I make a drying-room for hanging clothes," she wrote in a letter. But she loved the sweeping view toward the river—the view George Washington had chosen.

Then Thomas Jefferson moved into the President's House. He began traditions that would continue for many years. Jefferson wanted people to feel that the house belonged to them, as well as to the president who lived there. He opened the house so that people could visit the state rooms. Each Fourth of July, he staged a party on the grounds, complete with music played by the Marine Band.

Jefferson started a tradition of making changes to the President's House that would continue. James Madison and his wife, Dolley, ordered beautiful new furniture. They were the only first family ever to have to leave the house because of war. In 1814, during the War of 1812, British troops invaded Washington and set fire to the house. Only a few hours before the British arrived, Dolley Madison ordered that the Gilbert Stuart portrait of President Washington be removed from its frame. Two gentlemen from New York who had volunteered to help as she was preparing to flee took the painting and kept it safe. But almost everything else in the house was lost in the terrible fire. At daybreak only a hollow, blackened shell remained.

After the war ended, the President's House was rebuilt, using parts of the original walls. It took only three years to have the house ready. When President James Monroe was inaugurated in 1817, the carpenters had begun the inside work. When the new president moved in

Hang it up. In this painting, First Lady Abigail Adams watches as a servant hangs the laundry in the East Room of the spacious, but unfinished, President's House.

Father of his country. This life-size portrait of President George Washington was nearly lost during the War of 1812. It hangs in the East Room today.

later that year, bright white walls once again welcomed the first family.

Important changes and additions to the house were made in the nineteenth century. James Monroe added the South Portico in 1824. In 1829-30, Andrew Jackson added the North Portico, where visitors still arrive at the White House today. James K. Polk installed gas lighting in 1848, although his wife refused to have the newfangled system installed in the Blue Room chandelier. In the 1850s, Franklin Pierce had hot and cold water piped into the upstairs bathrooms and James Buchanan added a greenhouse.

During the Civil War, the President's House became the headquarters for Abraham Lincoln. Soldiers marched on the South Lawn and even camped in the East Room. When the war ended,

the house was illuminated outside with thousands of candles balanced on its windowsills. Tragically, Lincoln was assassinated a few days later, plunging the nation into grief. Lincoln's funeral was held in the East Room.

After the Civil War, presidents continued to change the house. Ulysses S. Grant added a billiard room. Rutherford B. Hayes installed the first telephone. Chester A. Arthur found the house so old-fashioned that he wanted to tear it down! Luckily, Congress, which had to approve money for the house, did not agree. Instead, Arthur got money to renovate the house, and added a vast stained-glass screen by Louis Comfort Tiffany in the Entrance Hall. Benjamin Harrison installed electric lights in 1891— although he and his wife were afraid to touch the switches. The stage was set for the twentieth century, when the White House would be not only a home, an office, and a ceremonial site, but also a living museum of our nation's history.

The Lincolns at home. In this imaginative portrait, President Abraham Lincoln, his wife, Mary, and their sons look relaxed and happy to be in the White House. The Capitol is shown in the distance—although it is not visible from the White House.

A Modern Mansion: The 20th Century

A vigorous new president entered the White House early in the new century. He was Theodore Roosevelt. He brought his large family of six children, ranging in age from three to sixteen, not to mention their various pets. The White House was too small for his lively family. In 1902, to make more room in the family quarters, the president moved staff offices from the second floor into an addition attached to the west side of the White House. It was called the Executive Office Building. Although Roosevelt intended this addition to be temporary, it grew larger and today is commonly known as the West Wing. However, Roosevelt continued to work in an upstairs study in the White House. In 1901,

Roosevelt made the popular name "White House" the official name of the mansion. He also extensively remodeled the White House, adding a new grand staircase, enlarging the State Dining Room, and changing the décor in every room.

In 1909, Roosevelt's successor, William Howard Taft, moved his office into the West Wing. He built the first Oval Office there.

Although rooms were redecorated and gardens were expanded by the first families that followed Taft, few major structural changes took place. In the 1920s, Calvin Coolidge raised the roof and added a steel and concrete third floor. Herbert Hoover had to rebuild the West Wing after a fire there in 1929. President Franklin D. Roosevelt tripled the West Wing office space by adding basement offices and a second floor.

But no renovation was as dramatic as the work done when Harry S. Truman was president. After the fire in 1814, the White House had been rebuilt with wooden framing, not a material that would last through the centuries. Over time, through many renovations and heavy use, the White House began to wear out. President Truman's daughter Margaret liked to play her grand piano, which was kept in her sitting room upstairs.

American animals. President Theodore Roosevelt decorated the State Dining Room with moose heads and other trophies of animals native to America. He even had carved lion heads on the mantelpiece refashioned into bison heads!

Construction zone. During Harry S. Truman's administration, the White House was gutted and a new, safer steel frame was installed. The original walls were preserved.

television shows made people around the United States more interested in the White House than ever before.

In 1961, an act of Congress made all historic White House objects part of a permanent museum collection. Mrs. Kennedy helped found the White House Historical Association, a nonprofit organization that publishes books and conducts research about the White House and raises funds to acquire and preserve significant objects for it.

One day the leg of the piano broke right through the floor! The house was inspected and found to be unsafe. The Trumans moved across the street to Blair House, a residence now used for visiting dignitaries. The White House was almost completely gutted.

Steel framing was put in to hold up the heavy walls that Washington had ordered built. Closets and storage rooms were added. When the Trumans returned in 1952, the president presented a televised tour of the renovated building. In 1962, First Lady Jacqueline Kennedy hosted another popular tour of the state rooms in the White House after historic room designs she directed were complete. These

In person. Mrs. Jacqueline Kennedy redecorated the State Rooms in the White House using historic objects and American antiques. The nation saw the new look in magazine articles and a televised tour.

The White House
TODAY and Tomorrow

President George W. Bush and his wife, Laura Bush, moved into the White House on January 20, 2001. Later that year, on September 11, tragedy struck the United States when terrorists flew two passenger jets into the Twin Towers of the World Trade Center in New York City and crashed another plane into the Pentagon in Virginia. A fourth plane, perhaps aimed at the White House, crashed in Pennsylvania.

Thousands of innocent people were killed. Since that terrible event in our history, public access to the White House has been limited. But President and Mrs. Bush—like other presidents as far back as Thomas Jefferson— want to keep the house available to the public. It is, as President Bush says, the people's house. Since six months after September 11, 2001, students and other organized youth groups have been welcomed back into the White House. There visitors see the portrait of President George Washington rescued by Dolley Madison, the impressive State Dining Room enlarged by Theodore Roosevelt, and the historic objects that fill every room with memories of our nation's history. They also see, as George Washington did in 1791, a view stretching toward the Potomac River.

Welcome to the White House. Both the North Portico (above) and the South Portico (right) welcome visitors such as Mexico's President Vicente Fox. An aerial photograph gives a clear view of the mansion set in its acres of grounds, surrounded by the busy capital city (far right). This is the view the president sees as he flies home in Marine One.

A Big Backyard:
The President's Park

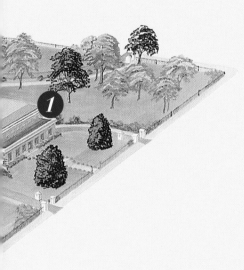

The eighteen and a half acres of grassy lawns and peaceful flower gardens around the White House make up the "President's Park." This painting of the White House grounds is based on an aerial photograph and a plan drawn by the National Park Service. It shows the extent of the green haven in the middle of a busy city. The oldest tree living in President's Park is a magnolia thought to have been planted by Andrew Jackson in memory of his wife, Rachel. In modern times, presidents and first ladies have continued the tradition of planting a variety of American tree species to commemorate their time in the White House. In spring and fall, the public can visit the grounds during garden tours. If you go, don't miss the Children's Garden!

Some trees planted by presidents and first ladies:

1. White oak planted by Franklin D. Roosevelt

2. Saucer magnolias planted by John F. Kennedy

3. Japanese maple planted by Jimmy Carter

4. Willow oak planted by Ronald Reagan

5. Little leaf linden planted by George Bush

6. White dogwoods planted by Hillary Rodham Clinton

Inside the White House:
The CUTAWAY

This painting depicts a selection of important rooms in the White House. These are rooms that visitors see when they tour the mansion. Groups enter from the east side of the house, stopping first at the Library. From there, they see the lovely portraits of first ladies in the Vermeil Room, learn about the various sets of White House china in the China Room, and then climb a marble stairway to the State Floor. Here they see the East Room, where so many historic events have happened. Next, they stroll through the Green Room, enjoying its American paintings. In the Blue Room, make sure you take a moment to glance out the window at the monuments in the distance. Since 1800, presidents and first ladies have greeted guests in the Blue Room. In the Red Room, admire the portrait of Dolley Madison and the American landscape paintings. Finally, enter the State Dining Room and imagine yourself sitting down to dinner with the president, first lady, and their important guests.

1. Library

2. Vermeil Room

3. China Room

4. East Room

5. Green Room

6. Blue Room

7. Red Room

8. State Dining Room

9. Diplomatic Reception Room

FACES &
VOICES *Betty C. Monkman, Curator Emeritus*

Betty Monkman had an important job for many years: to make sure that the 30,000 objects that belong to the White House are catalogued, cared for, used correctly, exhibited, and interpreted. As in a museum, the objects are carefully researched and preserved so that the stories they tell will always be available to the American people. Ms. Monkman knows a lot about the pieces in the White House. She worked in the Curator's Office from 1967 to 2002 and is the author of *The White House: Its Historic Furnishings and First Families,* as well as other publications about the Executive Mansion. We talked to her in her book-lined office in the basement of the White House shortly before she retired.

"I was hired to do research when Lady Bird Johnson was first lady," Ms. Monkman remembers. (President Lyndon Johnson had created a permanent Office of the Curator in 1964.)

Ms. Monkman was a history major in college. While working in the White House, she returned to school and earned a master's degree in American studies, with an emphasis in museum studies.

"Our office deals with the preservation of the

Betty C. Monkman stands in the State Dining Room. Beside her is one of the historic objects she was responsible for researching and keeping safe—a silver gilt wine cooler.

house and the historic objects," she says. "We make decisions about paintings and furnishings. We consider objects to be acquired by the White House—paintings or drawings or historic photographs."

The curators also work with the Secret Service officers who conduct tours for White House visitors, consult with an advisory committee about changes to the public rooms in the White House, and work on exhibits for the White House Visitor Center. The staff meet with individuals who want to donate historic materials to the house, as well.

When a new presidential family arrives at the White House, the Curator's Office provides information so they can choose historic objects to furnish their private quarters and the Oval Office. Amy Carter, who was eight years old when she moved in, chose a Grandma Moses painting of a Fourth of July picnic for her bedroom. President and Mrs. George W. Bush chose paintings of Texas for the Oval Office.

The White House may be a museum, but children who live there are allowed to choose the color of paint for their room and arrange the

furniture as they like. "When Chelsea Clinton was a teenager, she put up posters in her room, like any teenager," Ms. Monkman recalls.

"When I try to explain what a curator does, I remind kids that they collect things, too. Here we collect, organize, and take care of objects that have to do with the presidents and the White House. We see this house as a museum of America."

What is her favorite spot in the White House?

"I like the Lincoln Bedroom," Betty Monkman says. "We have the Gettysburg Address written in Lincoln's hand. In this house you get a sense of connection with past presidents from all the objects that we have."

The Lincoln Bedroom contains furniture, artwork, and a signed copy of the Gettysburg Address from President Abraham Lincoln's era. Guests of the president stay here.

The VISITOR Center

Welcome to Washington. Mrs. Laura Bush speaks at the opening of an exhibit on White House holiday decorations.

In March 1995, First Lady Hillary Rodham Clinton opened a new White House Visitor Center near the White House. The center, operated by the National Park Service, provides information to people who come to Washington, D.C., to see the city's important monuments. With its exhibits, lectures, and videos about the White House, the White House Visitor Center is an important resource for people touring the nation's capital.

The Visitor Center is located in the Great Hall of the Department of Commerce. It is open from 7:30 A.M. until 4 P.M. every day except Thanksgiving, Christmas, and New Year's Day. The center features

Go this way. A National Park Service ranger shows visitors a brochure about the White House tour.

The first residents. Actors playing Abigail and John Adams perform at the celebration of the 200th anniversary of the White House.

exhibits and information about many aspects of the White House, including its architecture, furnishings, first families, and social and diplomatic events. In 2002, for example, the center hosted an exhibit about the 100-year history of the West Wing, where the president and his staff do their work. If you drop in you might hear a lecture on First Lady Eleanor Roosevelt, listen to a Navy Band concert, watch a video about the president's travels on *Air Force One,* or pick up free tickets for one of the spring or fall garden tours of the beautiful White House grounds.

Exploring the exhibits. Visitors enjoy an exhibit on first families.

A Model White House

Views of the rooms. Visitors surround the model White House when it is on exhibit around the United States.

Crowds of people who have never visited the White House in person have been able to see it anyway—on a smaller scale. Model builder John Zweifel and his wife Jan, of Orlando, Florida, began construction of the model White House in 1962. The model is built on a scale of one inch to one foot, and is an exact replica of the White House, both inside and out. The recreation includes every detail, down to tiny working TV sets, miniature crystal chandeliers, paintings, carpets, and tableware.

Here's my house! First Lady Barbara Bush admires the model White House. She points out the Yellow Oval Room where many presidential families have enjoyed spending private time with friends.

The model shows three floors of the mansion, and includes the East and West Wings. The Zweifels' house has toured all fifty states and has been exhibited at the Smithsonian Institution in Washington, D.C., as well as the John F. Kennedy, Ronald Reagan, and George Bush Presidential Libraries. An estimated 42 million people have peered through its windows into the Red Room and checked out the miniature silverware and china in the State Dining Room, which is all set up for a party. Mr. Zweifel and his wife have spent more than thirty-five years lovingly building and decorating their replica of the president's house. They say the model is their "gift to the people." It is sixty feet long by twenty feet wide, and weighs more than ten tons.

A closer look. A visitor peers through a window to look at the detailed miniatures in the Red Room. Each piece in the White House model is a replica of a real White House object.

Mr. Zweifel believes his White House is the largest miniature house in the world. But the Zweifels never finish with their house. They keep in touch with White House staff about what may be changing in the mansion. Then every replica of a new furnishing and decoration has to be carved, painted, or sewn by hand. It is a lot of work!

Cutaway view. Each room in the White House is easy to see from the back of the model, which has no exterior walls. Viewers get a good look at the three levels of oval rooms that form the heart of the house.

On Saturday, November 1, 1800, John Adams arrived at the White House, becoming the first president to live in the building. That afternoon, his office was set up, and he went right to work. The White House became the place where the nation's business was conducted, as well as a place to live. Since then, the White House has been the center of the executive branch of the government.

KING
at the White House

Ready to work. The Oval Office of President George W. Bush includes the Resolute *desk, used by most presidents since 1880.*

Working ★ 46

The president has a big job—perhaps the biggest job in the world. He is responsible for seeing that U.S. laws are carried out. He guides American foreign policy as our chief diplomat and serves as commander in chief of the armed forces. Most of the many, many tasks involved in these jobs take place right in the White House, just as they did in John Adams's day.

Until 1902, when Theodore Roosevelt built the West Wing and moved most of his staff there, the nation's business was done in the residence. Thomas Jefferson used the space that is now the State Dining Room as his office. Andrew Jackson, like the nineteenth-century presidents who

followed him, put his offices upstairs next to the family quarters. Jackson's Cabinet, and those of succeeding nineteenth-century presidents, met upstairs as well.

Each president has had his own work style. Millard Fillmore, who served from 1850 to 1853, kept his White House office open seven days a week. Abraham Lincoln continued this practice during the Civil War.

Today, most of the administration's official business goes on in the East and West Wings, as well as in additional offices in the Eisenhower Executive Office Building next door and the New Executive Office Building nearby. The president works in the Oval Office in the West Wing, a spacious room that echoes the shape of the Blue Room.

A household staff works in the White House residence. In the 1840s, James K. Polk established a room at the front door where a White House employee registered visitors before they were ushered upstairs. This was necessary because so many people flooded the White House seeking jobs in the government that it was hard to control the crowd! Office-seekers lounged around on the furniture, talked, and spit tobacco juice into spittoons lining the hallways. (Office-seekers finally disappeared from the White House in 1883 when Civil Service examinations began to be used to match people with government jobs.)

Important calls. As President George Bush makes one call from his Oval Office desk, General Colin Powell makes another—from a phone tucked away in a bottom drawer.

The room President Polk set up, located to the right of the North Portico entrance, remains the White House Usher's Office today. From it, the chief usher runs the household, orchestrating the tasks of the ninety-five people who keep the modern White House residence running smoothly as the president goes about the business of leading the country.

A new wing. In 1902, President Theodore Roosevelt moved his staff into the brand new Executive Office Building, a simple, one-story addition painted white to match the mansion. A messenger's bicycle leans against the outside wall. In those days, visitors could walk right up to the building.

The
WESTWing

When President Theodore Roosevelt moved into the White House with his large family in 1901, the second floor had only eight rooms for his family—and just a few more were available as offices for the president and his staff. The business of the country went on right down the hall from the family's space, leaving them very little privacy. President Roosevelt asked Congress for funds for a major renovation, including the construction of an office addition to the White House so that his staff could move away from the family quarters.

In 1902, a New York architect, Charles F. McKim, oversaw the renovations and designed a suite of offices on the west side of the White House. This building, which connects to the White House through a colonnade built by Thomas Jefferson, is called the Executive Office Building, but has come to be called the West Wing. President Theodore Roosevelt did not move his official office to the new building; his study remained on the second floor. But the next president, William Howard Taft, did move his workspace over to the West Wing.

On Christmas Eve, 1929, during Herbert Hoover's presidency, the West Wing was damaged by fire. President Hoover rebuilt the space and continued to use it through his presidency.

During World War II, the number of people working in the West Wing grew to 225, making

Presidential pose. President Jimmy Carter talks to a visitor in the Oval Office. A bust of Benjamin Franklin stands on a chest behind him. Each president selects his own Oval Office furnishings—including art and sculpture.

the space very crowded even though President Franklin D. Roosevelt had expanded it early in his presidency. Today, about 150 staff members work for the president in the West Wing and first lady in the East Wing of the White House—and the space is still crowded and busy. The president arrives at his office simply by walking through the colonnade from the White House next door.

In addition to the Oval Office, today's West Wing houses the Cabinet Room, the Roosevelt Room, the Press Room, the office of the vice president, and many other offices. Much of the president's—and the nation's—most important business goes on there.

Situation Room. President George Bush and his staff talk over important matters during the Gulf War. This meeting room in the West Wing is reserved for use during important events or crises.

Oval playroom. John Kennedy Jr. often visited his father in the Oval Office, where he could play under the Resolute desk.

The OVAL Office

In 1934, President Franklin D. Roosevelt moved the Oval Office to the southeast corner of the expanded West Wing, overlooking the Rose Garden. It remains there today. In this room, the president meets with visiting chiefs of state, heads of government, and members of Congress and conducts other important business.

When a new president arrives at the White House, he chooses his Oval Office furnishings from among the historic possessions that belong to the house. Each president puts his own personal stamp on the room. President Harry S. Truman put a famous sign on his Oval Office desk. It said, THE BUCK STOPS HERE. Truman meant that he was the final person

responsible for decisions made by his administration. President John F. Kennedy, who served in the U.S. Navy and loved the sea, hung seascapes and naval scenes on the walls, and placed ship models on the tables. President Kennedy loved to play with his young children, Caroline and John, in the Oval Office. President Bill Clinton displayed busts of Franklin D. Roosevelt and Abraham Lincoln, along with family photos, on a table behind his desk. President George W. Bush has chosen paintings of Texas for his Oval Office.

Many modern presidents, including John F. Kennedy, Jimmy Carter, Ronald Reagan, Bill Clinton, and George W. Bush, have chosen

Photo opportunity. Susan Ford takes pictures of her father, President Gerald Ford.

to use a desk that was presented as a thank-you gift to President Rutherford B. Hayes by England's Queen Victoria in 1880. The desk is made of oak timbers from the HMS *Resolute,* a British ship that was saved by American whalers after it was marooned in Arctic ice. In 1945, a carved panel depicting part of the Presidential Seal was added to the *Resolute* desk at the suggestion of President Franklin D. Roosevelt. This desk dominates the Oval Office today. The décor of the Oval Office may change with each new president, but the flags standing behind the desk remain in their traditional places: the Presidential flag to the president's left and the U.S. flag to his right.

Thoughtful pause. National Security Adviser Condoleezza Rice looks out an Oval Office window as her boss, President George W. Bush, takes a phone call.

The CABINET Room

Matters of state. During a Cabinet meeting, President John F. Kennedy (right center) and Vice President Lyndon Johnson (left center) listen during a discussion. A portrait of President Abraham Lincoln looks down from the Cabinet Room wall.

Every president appoints a group of advisers to help him carry out his responsibilities. Called the Cabinet, this group is made up of the secretaries of the 15 government departments, such as the Department of State, the Department of Energy, and the Department of the Treasury. Cabinet secretaries are appointed by the president but must be approved by the Senate. There is no official schedule for Cabinet meetings, but most presidents assemble their Cabinet regularly.

The term "cabinet" comes from an Italian word, *cabinetto,* which means a small, private room—a good place for important discussions to take place. Before President Theodore Roosevelt built the West Wing in 1902, important Cabinet discussions took place in the White House itself. Then they moved to the West Wing. Since President Franklin D. Roosevelt's renovations in 1934, the Cabinet has assembled around a large conference table in a West Wing room that overlooks the Rose Garden. Each leather chair

bears a brass plaque with the title of the Cabinet member on it. Other important groups meet with the president in this room, as well, including the National Security Council and various congressional groups. Over the Cabinet Room mantelpiece hangs an inspiring painting (above), *The Declaration of Independence of the United States of America, July 4, 1776,* by French artist Charles Edouard Armand-Dumaresq.

The Cabinet Room today

Waiting for news. Sound movie trucks crowd around the North Portico of the White House in December 1929.

The PRESS Room

The White House has always attracted members of the press. Not only the president's political activities, but also his family, his pets, and his parties have generated millions and millions of words and thousands of photographs over the years. From 1902 through the late 1960s, a lobby in the West Wing served as a gathering place for the press. White House lore tells that President Theodore Roosevelt first invited reporters into the lobby when they were shivering outside in a winter storm. If you had visited the press lobby, you would have seen reporters and photographers crowding the room, sitting in worn leather armchairs as they waited for news to break.

In 1970, during President Richard Nixon's administration, the news media was moved to a Press Room built over President Franklin D. Roosevelt's indoor swimming pool, between the West Wing and the Residence. This area contains a briefing room where the president or his press secretary speaks to reporters and has booths for writers and broadcasters to use when they file their stories. Outside the West Wing is a graveled area on the lawn where TV crews set up their cameras. Today, some 100 reporters and photographers are assigned to cover the White House full-time and have clearance to work in the Press Room. They work for newspapers, wire services, and TV and radio stations from around the country and around the world.

Next question? In the Press Room, President Ronald Reagan speaks with newspaper, radio, and television reporters during a press conference.

Documenting history. While Mrs. Laura Bush stands by, White House photographer Eric Draper prepares to take a photograph. White House photographers record the president's activities on a daily basis.

FACES &
voices *Eric Draper, the President's Photographer*

Wherever President George W. Bush goes, you are sure to see Eric Draper close by. Mr. Draper is the president's photographer. He and his colleagues in the White House Photo Office take photographs of the president as he moves through his days, whether he is signing a bill, meeting with the Cabinet, or playing with his dogs.

Mr. Draper began work at the White House with President Bush in January 2001. "I used to be a photojournalist with the Associated Press. I covered the presidential campaign for eighteen straight months, and at the end of it I thought working for the president would be a good opportunity."

Mr. Draper's background as a news photographer serves him well in the busy White House. "It's all a matter of being at the right place at the right time," he says. "I follow the president almost everywhere, from the beginning of his day to the end of his day. My day is as long as the president's day. I'm not done until he's done."

The White House photographers take thousands and thousands of images of the president, his staff, his visitors, and his family. "The first year we used more than 14,000 rolls of film," Mr. Draper says.

One of the photographer's favorite images comes from Inauguration Day. "When the president walked into the Oval Office on his first day as president, I went with him," he recalls. "There he and his father, the former president, were, together at the desk for the first time. And it was my first time in the Oval Office, too! It was hard to control my excitement and remember to take pictures."

The EAST Wing

The East Wing serves as an important entrance to the White House. School groups and other visitors on tour walk through the East Wing office building along a glass-enclosed hall overlooking the Jacqueline Kennedy Garden. Theodore Roosevelt built an East Wing pavilion in 1902 as a formal entry for social occasions. President Franklin D. Roosevelt built a new East Wing during World War II, adding office space, a movie theater, and a bomb shelter.

Much of the office space in the East Wing is devoted to the first lady and her staff. Many first ladies have used their prominent position to work for causes in which they believe. Jacqueline Kennedy became very interested in restoring the White House. She helped found the White House Historical Association in 1961 and was involved in the publication of the first guidebook about the house. Nancy Reagan promoted the Foster Grandparents Program and worked to combat drug use among America's young people.

Laura Bush, a former public school librarian, is interested in education. Like her mother-in-law, Barbara Bush, she is especially concerned about literacy—the ability to read and to understand what you read. Her national initiative, "Ready to

Planning her day. First Lady Eleanor Roosevelt (right) consults with her secretaries in her office in the Residence. Mrs. Roosevelt was busy during her 12 years in the White House. She delivered speeches, traveled around the world, and wrote a popular newspaper column, "My Day."

Read, Ready to Learn," stresses that America's children should begin reading books with adults long before beginning school. On September 8, 2001, Mrs. Bush launched the first National Book Festival, featuring authors from around the nation. Three days later, on September 11, the United States experienced the worst terrorist attacks on its soil in history. Since then, Mrs. Bush has focused her energy on helping the nation—especially children—through the healing process.

First lady calling. Rosalynn Carter maintained an office in the East Wing. During her time in the White House, Mrs. Carter had a strong interest in programs to aid mental health.

FACES&
VOICES *Noelia Rodriguez, Press Secretary to the First Lady*

Noelia Rodriguez never expected to work in the White House. For one thing, she is a Democrat and the Bushes are Republicans. She already had an interesting and important job as deputy mayor of Los Angeles. Then Laura Bush called. She had heard what a good job Ms. Rodriguez had done working on a huge national convention—the Democratic Convention! Mrs. Bush decided she wanted Ms. Rodriguez on her staff no matter which party she belonged to.

"The press secretary is the spokesperson for the first lady," Ms. Rodriguez says. "My job is to be the link between Mrs. Bush and the press corps." The press secretary spends a lot of time helping Mrs. Bush prepare to talk to reporters and helping reporters prepare to talk to Mrs. Bush. "We have freedom of speech here in America, so reporters are at liberty to ask anything they want," Ms. Rodriguez says. "My job is to make sure everyone is ready with the information they need

to talk about the issues Mrs. Bush cares about— especially issues relating to children and their education in the early years."

When Mrs. Bush travels, Ms. Rodriguez goes along. Working and traveling with Mrs. Bush is exciting. "You get to work with the people you see on TV. I've even had my picture taken with Muhammad Ali! I've also had the honor of meeting Pope John Paul II while traveling with President and Mrs. Bush in Italy. But the best part is getting to work with Mrs. Bush directly. And going by the Oval Office and seeing the president never loses its magic.

"But the real magic for me was when the president and first lady invited my mom and me to Camp David for Thanksgiving. When I was a little girl, I never dreamed of going to the White House—let alone having Thanksgiving with the president and his family."

Setting the table. White House butlers prepare the State Dining Room for an event during President George Bush's administration. Historic china is used for formal events at the White House.

The RESIDENCE

Ready for guests. A housekeeper prepares a guest room in the upstairs area of the White House, where the first family entertains privately. This photo was taken during President Lyndon Johnson's time in the White House.

Dinner in 1900. President William McKinley often used the smaller Family Dining Room, next door to the State Dining Room. In this photo waiters set the table.

The White House has been the home of the president and his family for more than two centuries. Things have changed since Abigail Adams hung up her laundry in the East Room. Today the chief usher, who directs a staff of almost one hundred workers, oversees the everyday maintenance of the house, as well as the special jobs that need to be done for big events like State Dinners and holiday celebrations. And the laundry never hangs in the state rooms!

Keeping everything running smoothly in the Residence—the main White House building, which consists of the ground floor, State Floor, and the first family's private quarters—is a big job. After all, there are 132 rooms in the Executive Mansion. Floors need to be polished. Chandeliers need to be dusted. (One employee hand-cleans the three chandeliers in the East Room each year—which means handling more than 6,000 pieces of cut glass.) Carpets need to be vacuumed. Antique clocks need to be wound. Electrical and heating systems need to be maintained. Meals need to be prepared and served. Flowers need to be arranged and displayed. The grounds need to be planted, weeded, mowed, and raked.

Just a taste. In the White House kitchen, First Lady Nancy Reagan admires the handiwork of the White House chefs.

Moving day. Near the tradesmen's entrance into the ground floor of the White House, movers unload a truck filled with President Gerald Ford's belongings.

Rugs are rolled up and ropes are put up in preparation for White House tours. Then, when the tours end, the ropes are taken away, the oak floors are quickly polished, and the rugs are unrolled so the president and his family can use the house for ceremonies and receptions—or just to walk around in on their own.

Household staff members inside the White House are U. S. government employees, as are the National Park Service employees who work outdoors.

Some of the people who work in the White House remain there for their whole career, serving each president in turn. In fact, there are members of today's White House household staff who have worked there thirty years or more, including the maître d' and the White House electrician. Lillian Parks, a maid and seamstress, arrived during the Hoover administration in 1929 and stayed through the Eisenhower years, until 1960. Long service in the White House was a family tradition; Mrs. Parks's mother had been a maid for President and Mrs. William Howard Taft and stayed through President Franklin D. Roosevelt's terms.

Working in the White House is not like working anywhere else. The standards are high. Concerns about security and the first family's privacy are powerful. Many of the objects in the house are irreplaceable antiques and must be handled with special care. White House staffers also must be flexible. When a new president is elected, they have to say good-bye to a family they have known for years and get used to a new family's habits, likes, and dislikes. And the people who come to visit can be anyone from an eight-year-old Cub Scout to an Olympic athlete or even the Queen of England. Each visitor to the White House is treated with the same courtesy and respect.

Where else in the world can a nation's citizens so freely visit the home of their leader? Americans can feel quite protective of "their" house. Gary Walters, the chief usher, recalls that one tour operator who visited regularly scolded him gently about some fingerprints she had seen on a mirror for several weeks. Mr. Walters did not have the heart to tell her that what she called "smudges" were really worn sections on the surface of the 1815 mirror and had been there for many years. The household staff would never let fingerprint smudges remain on a White House mirror!

Rolling a rug. A workman arranges the carpet in the Blue Room. Before tour groups walk through the White House, carpets are moved out of the way. After the tours end, the rooms are set up again for the president's use.

FACES & VOICES
Roland Mesnier, Pastry Chef

Roland Mesnier is a pastry chef, but he's an artist, too. In a small pastry kitchen tucked upstairs in the White House, this French-born chef and his staff make beautiful and delicious cakes, cookies, chocolates, and other goodies for the president, his family, and his thousands of guests. Mr. Mesnier likes to create personalized decorations for his confections—from a chocolate bulldog to symbolize Yale, where President George W. Bush went to college, to a replica of a purple jeep for Chelsea Clinton's sixteenth-birthday cake.

Mr. Mesnier came to the White House in 1980, during the administration of Jimmy Carter. He had trained in France and had worked in several fine hotels before joining the White House staff.

"When we have a State Dinner here we don't just do a dessert," says Mr. Mesnier. "We try to do something that will show the visiting head of state that we did research about their country. That makes the dessert time fun. For every country or visiting dignitary we do something different." For example, for a State Dinner honoring India, Mr. Mesnier made a cake in the shape of a lotus flower. To decorate all the desserts that evening, Mr. Mesnier made 1,800 chocolate petals.

President George W. Bush's first big event was a dinner for all of the nation's governors, Mr. Mesnier recalls. "We did a dessert that looked like a Texas tumbleweed. We wanted to tell all our governors, 'The new president is from Texas. Don't forget it!'"

Mr. Mesnier says that the secret of success for a White House chef is to be fully dedicated to the family and to the house. He is available night and day, whether his job is to make a simple dessert that reminds the first family of home or a spectacular creation for a State Dinner.

"We can make a difference with the food," he says. "We not only feed the family, we also provide joy. A dessert can be a distraction from the daily grind and the astronomical responsibilities the president faces."

Presidential mints. Pastry chef Roland Mesnier's artistry created this chocolate box with a spun sugar flower, which holds chocolate mints embossed with the Presidential Seal.

SECURITY
at the White House

*Fore! As two Secret Service agents watch closely,
President Gerald Ford practices his golf game on the South Lawn.*

Today when the president leaves the White House, he rides in an armored car. That's quite different from the 1820s, when President John Quincy Adams enjoyed strolling by himself down the hill from the White House for a cooling dip in the Potomac River.

The world has changed dramatically since then, and so have the security concerns at the White House and in other places around the world.

Roll call. As the captain of the
Metropolitan police calls the roll,
President Theodore Roosevelt's
young sons stand at attention.
Later, this unit became the
White House police force.

two full-time agents were assigned
to the White House detail. Before
that, presidents relied on hired
guards in civilian clothes. In the 1840s, President
John Tyler established the first permanent
security force at the White House. Called
"doormen," these guards also helped out by
running errands and receiving callers. President
Franklin Pierce had a full-time bodyguard, paid
by the government. President Pierce never left
the White House by himself—a tradition that
continues into modern times.

By law, the modern Secret Service must remain
close to the president at all times, offering
protection without interfering with his ability
to communicate with people as he goes about his
daily routine. The Secret Service also guards the
president-elect, the vice president, their families,
and former presidents and first ladies.

Attention! On the South Lawn, President Harry S. Truman
poses with the members of the White House police force.

The days when anyone could wander into the
White House on New Year's Day—as they could
during every presidency through Herbert
Hoover's—are gone.

Armed, highly trained officers of the Executive
Protective Service, a branch of the Secret Service,
guard the president and his family wherever they
go, whether it is a shopping trip or a senior prom.
The Secret Service was given responsibility for
protecting the president in 1901, after President
William McKinley was assassinated. In 1902,

On alert. A member of the White House uniformed Secret Service
detailed to protect President George W. Bush scans Lafayette Park
from his post at the North Portico.

CELEB

RATING

at the White House

The White House has been a place for celebrations from the very beginning. Although he occupied the President's House for only four months, President John Adams was the first to entertain there. On January 1, 1801, he and his wife, Abigail, held a reception in the second-floor oval room with its view of the Potomac River. Thomas Jefferson would continue this tradition of the New Year's reception, and added an outdoor Fourth of July party complete with a concert by the Marine Band.

Sparkling nights. Gloria Estefan sings for President and Mrs. George Bush in 1991.

President James Madison and his wife, Dolley, entertained constantly. A New York senator wrote of Dolley Madison, "I never saw a lady who enjoyed society more than she does." In 1809, Mrs. Madison began to entertain as many as 200 people at receptions known as her "Wednesday drawing rooms." She served cake, ice cream, coffee, and wine. When the British marched into Washington and then into the President's House in August 1814, they found a table set for a festive dinner. Before they burned the house, the invaders helped themselves to the president's food and wine.

After the White House was rebuilt, President James Monroe began the New Year's receptions again on a sunny January 1, 1818. The house was packed with visitors from noon to 3 P.M. Paint was still drying on the walls of the rebuilt mansion! A New Year's reception for the public

remained a White House tradition for more than 130 years. President Abraham Lincoln signed the Emancipation Proclamation after the 1863 New Year's reception. A year later, on New Year's Day, 1864, a large group of African-American men and women arrived at the White House. They walked through the Blue Room to shake the president's hand. Until that day, people of color ordinarily had not been guests at the White House.

By the twentieth century, the New Year's crowds had become too large for the house and the president to handle. More than 6,000 people showed up in 1931! However, the first families have found many other ways to offer their hospitality, from elegant black-tie dinners in the State Dining Room to casual barbecues on the South Lawn. Presidents, first ladies—and their children—demonstrate their style and taste when they entertain. They have offered a showcase for talented, popular American performers, including Mary Chapin Carpenter, Gloria Estefan, Jon Bon Jovi, Regina Belle, and more.

Closed gatefold: Children fill the South Lawn for the annual White House Easter Egg Roll.

Open gatefold: An artist imagines a White House reception in Abraham Lincoln's East Room, with many famous guests of the Civil War period.

ARRIVALS and Departures

Transfer of power. In 1913, President William Howard Taft (at left) leaves the White House for the Capitol, where President-elect Woodrow Wilson (at right) will be sworn in.

Inaugural party. Andrew Jackson's time in the White House began with a large celebration that might have looked like this crowded 19th-century scene.

One of the most remarkable things about the United States is that power has passed peacefully from president to president since George Washington handed over the reins of government to John Adams. When a new president is elected and the former one leaves office, moving day arrives at the White House. The transfer of power from one president to another occurs at the inauguration ceremony.

At the same time, the transfer of household possessions happens at the White House as one family's things are moved out and another's moved in. The chief usher and his staff oversee this complicated operation while everyone else is at the Capitol watching as the new president is sworn in.

Welcome to your new home. (left) Mrs. Lyndon Johnson, Mrs. Richard Nixon, and their daughters Luci Johnson and Tricia Nixon, discuss life in the White House during the transition. (below left) President Gerald Ford's staff pack his personal belongings in the Oval Office. (below) President John F. Kennedy and a friend decide where to hang paintings in the Oval Office as Kennedy begins his new job as president.

On Inauguration Day in 1841, outgoing president Martin Van Buren received well-wishers in the East Room before walking down Pennsylvania Avenue to the Capitol to witness the swearing in of the new president, William Henry Harrison. In 1853, President-elect Franklin Pierce and President Millard Fillmore rode together to the Capitol for the ceremony. In 1869, however, the outgoing president, Andrew Johnson, who had become president when Abraham Lincoln was assassinated, did not stay in Washington for the inauguration. As he and his family climbed into carriages and traveled away from the White House, the band music of the inaugural parade honoring Civil War hero and new president Ulysses S. Grant could be heard in the distance.

In modern times, on Inauguration Day, the incoming president arrives at the North Portico and is met by the outgoing president. They travel together from the White House to the Capitol for the swearing-in ceremony. Their journey has become a powerful symbol of this nation's peaceful transfer of power from one person to another and often from one political party to another.

An outdoor party. On a mild May evening in 1979, President and Mrs. Jimmy Carter entertained the Prime Minister of Japan at a State Dinner set up on the West Terrace.

Honored guests. President and Mrs. John F. Kennedy prepare to enter a State Dinner with India's Prime Minister Jawaharlal Nehru and his daughter, Indira Gandhi.

STATE Dinners

Even before the White House was built, having dinner with the president of the United States was very special. In the President's House in Philadelphia, George Washington began the tradition of inviting government officials and other important people to dine with him.

White House events honor foreign visitors, allow important people to meet in a relaxed setting, and showcase the president and first lady as America's official host and hostess. Entertaining is part of their job. When heads of other nations come to the United States, a State Dinner is sometimes given at the

Your health, Your Majesty. President Gerald Ford toasts Great Britain's Queen Elizabeth II during her visit to the United States Bicentennial celebration in July 1976.

White House to celebrate their visit. State Dinners are formal occasions. Guests wear their best evening clothes. Tables are draped with tablecloths and set with beautiful flowers and historic White House china, glassware, and silver. A menu created by the White House calligrapher lists the fare for the evening.

President Franklin D. Roosevelt hosted one of the most famous State Dinners held in the White House. In 1939, King George VI and Queen Elizabeth I of England came to the United States, the first visit of a reigning British monarch. The king and queen paid a two-day call at the White House. (The room where Queen Elizabeth I slept is called the Queens' Bedroom to this day.) After a formal dinner, American folk songs were performed for the king and queen in the East Room. Later, the king and the president sat together and talked until early in the morning. It was the last great ceremonial event in the White House in the 1930s. A few months later, Great Britain would be at war; the United States would join the conflict two years after that.

The president's place. At a State Dinner, each place is set with fine china and silver and beautifully lettered place cards and menus.

The first State Dinner hosted by President and Mrs. George W. Bush honored Mexican President Vicente Fox. It was held in the State Dining Room, which seats 140 people. Guests dined at round tables, enjoying a meal that concluded with pastry chef Roland Mesnier's special Mexican-themed dessert, mango and coconut ice cream with red chili sauce.

Rose Garden CEREMONIES

A holiday honor. President Ronald Reagan signs a bill creating a holiday to remember Dr. Martin Luther King Jr. as Mrs. Coretta Scott King (left of President Reagan) looks on.

Workers for peace. In the Rose Garden, President John F. Kennedy speaks to the first group of Peace Corps volunteers. Kennedy founded the Peace Corps on March 1, 1961. The first volunteers served in Africa.

The beautiful Rose Garden's convenient setting and natural beauty make it the perfect place for White House ceremonies honoring individuals and groups of all kinds.

Roses were first planted in 1913 in this area next to the West Wing by Ellen Wilson, wife of President Woodrow Wilson. In 1962, the garden was redesigned and replanted at the request of President John F. Kennedy to create an outdoor setting for ceremonies and events. Flower beds divided by boxwood hedges surround a level, rectangular lawn with room for 1,000 guests. Crabapple trees are planted around the garden in neat rows. At any time of year except deep winter, something is in bloom in the Rose Garden: vivid tulips, scented roses and lilies, or bright chrysanthemums.

Hundreds of accomplished people have stood in this garden to be recognized by presidents over the years. President Kennedy saluted the first Peace Corps volunteers there before they left to serve poor communities in other countries. The first U.S. astronauts were honored there; so was the first woman to sit on the United States Supreme Court. Another kind of ceremony— a wedding—took place there when President Richard Nixon's daughter Tricia married Edward Finch Cox in June 1971.

President George W. Bush has made frequent use of the Rose Garden. There he celebrated the

FACES & VOICES
Irvin M. Williams, Grounds Superintendent

Irvin Williams has worked at the White House longer than any other member of the staff. He arrived as a part-time worker during the Truman administration. Then, in 1961, Jacqueline Kennedy asked that he work full-time—and he has been there just about every day since. When you are superintendent of grounds, there is always something to keep you busy, whether it is tending a magnolia tree believed to have been planted by President Andrew Jackson, fixing the lawn after thousands of children have rolled eggs across it on Easter Monday, keeping the squirrels from eating the tulip bulbs, or helping pick out the White House holiday tree.

The son of a West Virginia farmer, Mr. Williams knows every tree, shrub, and flower on the 18½ acres of White House grounds. He should! He

A favorite tree. Irvin Williams points out a magnolia tree, traditionally thought to have been planted by President Andrew Jackson, to young visitors to the White House grounds.

planted many of them. "Trees tie it all down," he says of the White House grounds.

Mr. Williams has always loved spending time with the president's children and grandchildren. "Caroline and John Kennedy would ride their ponies Macaroni and Tex on the lawn almost every day," he remembers.

World Series champions and congratulated the Teacher of the Year. In a moving Rose Garden ceremony on September 18, 2001—one week after September 11—President Bush honored representatives of the many volunteer organizations that were helping comfort and support victims and their families after the terrorist attacks on New York City and the Pentagon.

A happy couple. Mr. and Mrs. Edward Finch Cox leave the Rose Garden after their wedding in 1971. The bride, Tricia, is President Richard Nixon's older daughter.

Jazz man. Ninety-five-year-old pianist Eubie Blake plays for President and Mrs. Jimmy Carter and guests on the South Lawn.

Flying high. Leslie Bradley, a young member of the Joffrey Ballet, leaps with the South Portico as a backdrop.

Ceremonial dance. Native American dancers perform in the East Room.

Celebrating

The White House has provided a stage for many performers. Popular, as well as classical, music has often been heard in the halls of the White House. President and Mrs. Jimmy Carter started the tradition of broadcasting White House concerts. President and Mrs. Ronald Reagan also launched a series of televised concerts. Before the first concert, Mrs. Reagan said, "Ever since this wonderful house was built, it's been filled with music. Thomas Jefferson played his violin and Harry Truman his piano in [the East Room]." These "In Performance at the White House" concerts have continued. They are designed to give all Americans a chance to experience the great performances, making the White House, as Mrs. Reagan said, "a concert hall for the entire nation."

Many of the performers who appear in the White House are American, but some are international stars. President and Mrs. John F. Kennedy were famous for bringing many artists to the White House. Among them was the great cellist, Pablo Casals, who gave a concert in the East Room in 1961. (He had appeared at the White House before, playing for Theodore Roosevelt in 1904.) The Kennedy concert was broadcast on radio from the White House and was made into a record.

Since the Kennedys, presidents and first ladies have continued the tradition of bringing the best performers to the White House, whether it is the Boys Choir of Harlem or an international star like cellist Yo-Yo Ma. Being able to host great performers is one of the pleasures of life in the White House. In 1989, when President George Bush and his wife, Barbara, hosted Phong Sak Meunchanai, a young singer from Thailand, the president said, "Here at the White House we're very privileged—every president is—to have great artists come to this magnificent home, the people's home."

the ARTS

Solo artistry. Spanish cellist Pablo Casals played for the Kennedys and their guests in the East Room in 1961.

FACES & VOICES

Timothy W. Foley,
Director of the Marine Band

Colonel Timothy Foley is the twenty-sixth director of the United States Marine Band, a group known as "The President's Own." Created by an act of Congress in 1798, the Marine Band is the oldest musical organization in the United States. It has provided the music for every president since John Adams.

Colonel Foley has been with the band since 1968. "I took an audition as a clarinet player," he recalls. "My grandfather was a Marine, a survivor of the Spanish-American War. After enlisting in the Marine Corps he went right to Marine Barracks at Eighth and I streets in Washington, D.C., which is the oldest post in the Marine Corps and our headquarters. I had known about the Marine Band since I was a kid and was fascinated with it. It was by pure luck that at the time I was ready to graduate from college, there was a spot available and I got it. I was one of sixty clarinets auditioning for that vacancy!"

He has loved every minute of his career with the Marine Band. "It's a wonderful organization steeped in tradition," he says. "Our mission is to play for the president and the commandant of the Marine Corps. We do that and more."

Leader of the band. Colonel Timothy W. Foley of the U.S. Marine Band.

The Marine Band plays every day. "We rehearse in the morning, and in the afternoon we might do anything from an event at the White House to a ceremony at Arlington National Cemetery. We also give free concerts in the summertime at the Capitol and the Washington Monument grounds. We march in Friday night parades at the Marine Barracks."

The Marine Band plays during the White House fireworks display on the Fourth of July and for State Dinners. They also perform when foreign dignitaries arrive on the South Lawn, and at presidential inaugurations. "Our job is to provide the musical backdrop," Colonel Foley says.

The Marine Band plays and records just about every kind of music you can imagine. "I'm a trained classical musician, but I have to know country music, too. I have to know it all! We once even backed up Frank Sinatra in the East Room. Music for ballet, opera—you name it, we've done it."

Colonel Foley says he finds patriotic marches the most stirring. "My favorite is John Phillip Sousa's *The Stars and Stripes Forever.* You never get tired of it—it's great music. I can have tears in my eyes playing American music. The experience of conducting *The Star Spangled Banner* at the beginning of a concert is very powerful."

Ready to play. Marine Band trumpeters play "Hail to the Chief" to announce the entrance of a president (above). John Phillip Sousa (below center) was the first director of the Marine Band (below). This group portrait was taken in 1891.

Easter Egg ROLL

Ready, set, roll! Kids try to win an egg race on the White House lawn (left). Children dressed up for the Easter Egg Roll in 1922 (above).

Once a year the South Lawn of the White House turns into a playground. It's time for the Easter Egg Roll! This traditional event began in the late 1800s. In the beginning, the roll took place on the steep, sloping lawns of Capitol Hill. But Congress decided to close its grounds to use as "play grounds." In 1879, crowds of children turned up ready to roll on Capitol Hill—but they were sent away. They made their way to the White House, where President Rutherford B. Hayes welcomed them. The event has taken place on the South Lawn of the White House ever since, although it was sometimes suspended during the two World Wars.

The Egg Roll, hosted by the president and first lady, gets started early in the morning on Easter Monday. In recent years, as many as 28,000 people have shown up. The Egg Roll is a public event. Free tickets are distributed at the Visitor Center on the Saturday before Easter. Each ticket lists a time to arrive, but the lines are long! The South Lawn is crowded, but orderly, as the egg-rolling game gets going. The game involves moving a hard-boiled egg across the lawn with a kitchen spoon, to the accompaniment of much laughter and yelling! At the end of the event, everyone takes home a wooden egg as a souvenir.

FACES&
voices
Clare Pritchett,
Director of the Visitors Office

If you have been able to tour the White House with a school group recently, Clare Pritchett probably had something to do with getting you there. A Texas native, Ms. Pritchett joined the White House when President George W. Bush was elected. She had worked for him when he was the governor of Texas, and then worked with Mrs. Laura Bush during the presidential campaign.

"Our office is responsible for tours and special projects," she says. "We were very glad to open back up for school groups in February 2002 after the events of September 11. Mrs. Bush says she is happy to hear voices in the house again."

The excitement of working in the White House has not worn off yet. "It's amazing to come to work in the morning," Ms. Pritchett says. Inauguration Day was the first time she had ever been to the White House. She was so busy helping guests at the reviewing stand for the inaugural parade that the reality of where she was had not really sunk in. "It was a rainy, cold day," she recalls, "Suddenly I turned around and felt like I could reach out and touch the White House, it was so close. And I could just walk in the front door!

"I feel so privileged. Every day I come in through

Welcome! Clare Pritchett stands in the East Garden, next to the enclosed colonnade through which tours enter the White House.

the gates and I see people peering through, their hands on the fence, and I get to go in. You never really get used to it. It's too powerful to even grasp sometimes."

The Easter Egg Roll is the biggest project Ms. Pritchett works on. "It takes lots of planning," she says. "The eggs arrive at the White House the week before. About 11,000 eggs for the children are cooked and colored in the White House kitchen. We have about 400 volunteers to help at the event, and we need them all!"

WHITE HOUSE Holidays

Happy holidays! The president and first lady kick off the holiday season each year by lighting the National Christmas Tree, which stands tall on the Ellipse behind the White House.

Thousands of lights. A volunteer decorates a tree for the holidays in the Blue Room.

Holidays bring festive times to the White House. Ever since John Adams's New Year's Day reception in 1801, this has been a place where holidays are remembered and celebrated.

President Benjamin Harrison probably decorated the first White House Christmas tree for his grandchildren in 1889. The president gathered the White House servants and gave each one a Christmas turkey.

Today, the National Park Service locates and delivers an 18½-foot evergreen tree to the Blue Room. The tree is so tall that White House electricians remove the chandelier and wire the tree to the medallion in the ceiling so it will not topple over. Meanwhile, the gigantic National Christmas Tree can be seen glittering on the Ellipse—an oval park south of the White House—through the Blue Room windows. Its lights are turned on by the president or first lady each December to begin the holiday season.

The White House was the scene of a wild holiday party in 1903. Mrs. Theodore Roosevelt invited children who lived in Washington, D.C., to come over on the day after Christmas.

Hanukkah candles. As President George W. Bush looks on, a young girl lights the second candle on a Menorah to honor the Jewish holiday.

Five hundred and fifty children and adults listened to the Marine Band play carols. The children ate sweets and watched a dancing show. Then President and Mrs. Roosevelt allowed them to play in the East Room for the rest of the party! Today, there is a family holiday party for the White House residence staff in the White House each year. Kids may not get to run around in the East Room anymore, but they still have a lot of fun.

Many other festive times are observed throughout the year. Each summer, the spectacular Fourth of July fireworks displays are staged on the Mall in Washington, D.C. Until the 1930s, when crowds grew too large for safety, there was a public reception at the White House on the Fourth. Today, the first family often watches the show from the South Portico balcony, with its great view of the Washington Monument and other memorials, as hundreds of guests enjoy the view from the South Lawn.

At Thanksgiving, the president traditionally "pardons" a turkey, rescuing it from becoming someone's dinner. The lucky turkey is sent to live out its days at a petting zoo. This tradition first began in President Lincoln's time, when he

Pumpkin carving. Amy Carter (second from left) and friends carve jack-o-lanterns in the China Room. A white sheet protects the carpet!

spared Jack, his son Tad's pet turkey, from becoming Thanksgiving dinner. Years later, in 1947, President Harry S. Truman began the practice of pardoning a national Thanksgiving turkey. The tradition has gone on uninterrupted since then. In 2001, President George W. Bush pardoned a turkey named Liberty.

You're free! President Gerald Ford "pardons" a turkey on Thanksgiving Day. The bird was sent to live at a petting zoo.

Glorious Fourth. Fireworks explode in the sky near the White House, Washington Monument, and Jefferson Memorial on the Fourth of July.

WHITE HOUSE
Ornaments

In 1981, the White House Historical Association started a new holiday tradition—the annual White House holiday ornament. The very first White House ornament was an antique angel weathervane. Soon, the organization decided that each ornament should honor a president, beginning with George Washington and moving forward in chronological order. (Exceptions are made for important White House anniversaries. For the mansion's 200th anniversary in 2000, a special White House Bicentennial ornament was designed.)

White House ornaments are sold to the public, and cost about $15 each. Many people buy them every year. Different companies compete for the honor of designing the piece each season. The ornaments are very popular! Hundreds of thousands are sold every year. The money from ornament sales supports the programs of the White House Historical Association, including preservation of the public rooms in the White House.

Holiday cheer. The White House Historical Association issues a new ornament each year (clockwise from far left). In 1981, it depicted an 1840 angel weathervane. The 1983 version showed the original 1800 White House. In 1994, the Marine Band of President James K. Polk marched across the ornament. Lincoln graced the 1999 ornament. In 2000, a bicentennial ornament was created. In 1989, the bicentennial of the presidency was honored. The 2001 ornament featured a horse and carriage from President Andrew Johnson's era.

A White House Tour

ROOM

by

ROOM

In 1961, President Kennedy and his wife, Jacqueline, introduced a new way of thinking about the White House. Understanding that it contains important objects that tell the story of our nation, the first lady began an ambitious project to catalog the contents of the house and acquire additional objects. She and the president believed that the house should become a museum of the nation's heritage. But it is a living museum. Here, the president, his family, and his guests actually use the historic objects that surround them. History was made here in the past, is being made today, and will be made tomorrow and in the years to come.

Look closely. Visiting students learn about the history of the Blue Room from a tour officer.

Room by Room ★ 94

FACES & voices

Russ Appleyard, Tour Officer

Russ Appleyard, a tour officer with the Secret Service, recently retired after working at the White House for twenty years. Officers on the "tour detail" are responsible for guarding the state rooms of the White House as tours pass through— and for answering questions about the rooms where they stand.

"I arrived at work at six-thirty in the morning on a typical day," Officer Appleyard recalls. "We'd have roll call, and I would put the tour schedule together and go over the list of who would be in the White House that day. We had fifteen to twenty school groups each day—about seven hundred and fifty people."

The White House tour detail members undergo a two-week training in cooperation with the Office of the Curator to learn the history of the rooms. But the number-one question they are asked has nothing to do with portraits or porcelain. It is: "Is the president here?" Often, the answer is, "Yes, he's in his office." However, tourists rarely see the president, though they have caught glimpses of the first lady and the presidential dogs from time to time.

The second most common question is, "Are these rooms used?" It is not surprising that kids ask that, since the house looks so much like a

museum. But the answer is yes, Officer Appleyard says. "We tell kids, 'Once you guys are out of the house we bring in dogs and an explosives team to check everything. When the house is declared safe, the usher sends out workers who roll the rugs back down. Then the president of the United States and the first lady have their house back.'"

Officer Appleyard's day did not end when the tours were over. The men and women on his team also work at all White House social events. Officer Appleyard saw wonderful things at those events during his two decades in the White House. Perhaps his favorite moment was watching actor John Travolta dance with Diana, Princess of Wales, in 1985. "They danced to 'Disco Inferno,'" he says. "That was a dinner unlike most other State Dinners."

Tour officers provide information to visitors. They are also responsible for protecting the White House.

The LIBRARY

Visitors begin their White House tour on the east side of the building. They walk down a long, glassed-in hallway to the Ground Floor Corridor. Portraits of first ladies hang on the wall and busts of presidents stand on pedestals. There are several important rooms along this hallway. One of them is the Library. Here, a collection of 2,700 books written by American authors, or about American history, lines the walls. The first White House library was begun by Abigail Fillmore in the upstairs oval room in the family quarters. The Library was relocated downstairs in 1935 by Franklin D. Roosevelt. White House staff and the president's family can check out books from this collection anytime. Amy Carter, who was in third grade when she moved into the White House, sometimes used the books to do research for her homework. Interesting portraits hang on the Library walls, including four depicting Native American emissaries who visited the White House in 1822, when James Monroe was president. He is remembered for the Monroe Doctrine, a position the president took stating that no European nation could seek colonies in the Western Hemisphere.

American literature. The books lining the shelves of the White House Library are by American authors or on American topics. Mrs. Laura Bush is sometimes filmed here for television broadcasts.

The VERMEIL Room

Sometimes called the Gold Room, this room was refurbished in 1991. The walls of the Vermeil Room are a shade of yellow, to complement a collection of vermeil, or gilded silver, that was received by the White House in 1957. Pieces from this collection are sometimes used on the State Floor. During receptions the room is used as a ladies' sitting room. It contains portraits of several twentieth-century first ladies. A portrait of Lady Bird Johnson wearing a gold-colored gown hangs over the mantelpiece. In the background, artist Elizabeth Shoumatoff included the Jefferson Memorial, a reminder of Mrs. Johnson's favorite view from the White House. Patricia Ryan Nixon's portrait

by Henrietta Wyeth hangs here, as well.

On the south wall is a full-length portrait of Jacqueline Kennedy painted by Aaron Shikler, who also painted a full-length portrait of First Lady Nancy Reagan. Mrs. Reagan was a great admirer of Jacqueline Kennedy, although their husbands were from opposing political parties. When it came time to have her portrait painted, Mrs. Reagan chose the same artist. An interesting portrait of Eleanor Roosevelt also hangs in this room. It shows several different views of Mrs. Roosevelt's face and hands, as she is knitting, gesturing, and holding eyeglasses. Painter Douglas Chandor used the technique to capture the energetic first lady's many moods.

"Wild Turkey." President and Mrs. Rutherford B. Hayes ordered a set of china showing American animals and plants.

The CHINA Room

E dith Wilson, who married President Woodrow Wilson after his first wife Ellen died, established the China Room to house the White House's collection of historic china, glassware, and silver. A dramatic portrait by Howard Chandler Christy of First Lady Grace Coolidge with her dog Rob Roy hangs in the room and suggests the room's red color scheme. Glass-fronted cabinets display presidential china patterns, including the latest set selected by Hillary Rodham Clinton for the 200th anniversary of the White House in 2000. Most presidents and first ladies are represented in the White House china collection,

starting with George and Martha Washington. Patriotic symbols, especially the American eagle, appear on many of the plates and other pieces. The famous and unusual Rutherford B. Hayes service, made in 1880 by the French manufacturer Haviland & Co., is painted with American plants and a menagerie of American animals, including a platter showing a strutting wild turkey. Lady Bird Johnson's design features American wildflowers. For many years, presidential china was manufactured in France or England. But beginning with the Wilson administration, the china has been made in America.

The best dishes. Sets of china from many different administrations are displayed here.

The Diplomatic Reception Room

"Views of North America." This rare 19ᵗʰ-century wallpaper depicts scenes from early America.

One of the views shown on the wallpaper is of Boston's waterfront.

Fireside chat. President Franklin D. Roosevelt often broadcasted radio addresses from the Diplomatic Reception Room.

This oval room has been used when foreign ambassadors arrive to present their credentials to the president. It offers a convenient entrance from the South Portico, so the first family often exits and enters the White House through this room. President Franklin D. Roosevelt used this space to broadcast his famous "Fireside Chats" over the radio. But the room has not always been used in such an official way; in the past, the White House furnace and boiler were located there. In 1960, the Eisenhowers furnished the oval room as a drawing room, using antique furniture made by American craftsmen. Mrs. John F. Kennedy added the panoramic wallpaper, titled "Views of North America," that was manufactured in France about 1834. During her restoration of White House decorations and furnishings, she heard that panels of the paper had been removed from an old house in Maryland, and she arranged to have them donated to the White House. The wallpaper shows landscapes of the Natural Bridge of Virginia, Niagara Falls, New York Bay, West Point on the Hudson River, and Boston Harbor. This scenic paper was very popular in the United States when Andrew Jackson was president in the 1830s.

The Entrance Hall & the Cross Hall

Tiffany glass. President Chester A. Arthur had a red-white-and-blue stained-glass screen installed in the Entrance Hall.

Come upstairs now to the State Floor of the White House. Opening into the Entrance Hall is the Grand Staircase, used on very special occasions. The seals of the original thirteen states are carved into the staircase archway. Standing in the Entrance Hall, a visitor can look through the windows of the oval Blue Room and see the Washington Monument and Jefferson Memorial. Perpendicular to the Entrance Hall is the Cross Hall. This hall stretches from the East Room to the State Dining Room, and the Red, Blue, and Green Rooms open into it. The Presidential Seal is set above the Blue Room door. In these two halls hang portraits of twentieth-century presidents, including Franklin Roosevelt, John F. Kennedy, Lyndon Johnson, Gerald Ford, Jimmy

Presidential Seal. Flags flank the door to the Blue Room, in the center of the White House. The Presidential Seal is positioned above it.

Carter, Ronald Reagan, and George Bush. This space has not always looked as open and spacious as it does today. In 1882, President Chester A. Arthur installed a red-white-and-blue stained-glass screen between the columns that spanned the width of the Entrance Hall. It was the first thing visitors saw when they entered. The screen was taken down during the Theodore Roosevelt renovation in 1902 and sold at auction.

Red carpet. The president can make a grand entrance into the East Room by walking down the Cross Hall.

The EAST Room

Sad times. The body of President Warren Harding lies in state in the East Room after he died in 1923 during a trip to California

If these walls could talk, what a tale they would tell! The East Room has probably witnessed more history than any other space in the White House. The portrait of George Washington that hangs on the East Room wall is the only object known to have remained in the White House since 1800. The portrait escaped burning when First Lady Dolley Madison ordered it taken down in 1814, when the White House was burned by British troops.

The East Room is the biggest room in the White House and was designed for large gatherings. There have been hundreds of them over the years. Presidential press conferences have been held here; the daughters of Ulysses S. Grant, Theodore Roosevelt, and Lyndon Johnson were married here. Theatrical perfomances have been held here. There has even been a senior prom, hosted by Susan Ford,

President Gerald Ford's daughter—with 100 percent attendance!

The East Room has also been a scene of sorrow. After the assassinations of Abraham Lincoln and John F. Kennedy, the presidents' coffins rested here. Seven presidents who died in office have lain in here as citizens mourned.

Union troops camped on the East Room floor briefly during the Civil War, when the nearby Confederate army threatened the capital city. Presidents have signed important bills into law beneath the glittering East Room chandeliers— including the Civil Rights Act, signed into law by President Lyndon Johnson on July 2, 1964.

The color green has dominated this room, one of three parlors named for colors on the State Floor of the White House, since Thomas Jefferson had a canvas floor cloth here that was painted green. Jefferson ate dinner here. President James Monroe used the parlor as a card room and furnished it with green silk drapes and upholstery fabrics. The Green Room was completely refurbished in 1971, during the Nixon administration. Today, most of the American-made furniture in the room dates from 1800–1815, and small teas and meetings are held here. Several examples of the White House collection of American art hang in the Green Room, including John Singer Sargent's *The Mosquito Net* and *Mountain at Bear Lake—Taos,* a landscape by Georgia O'Keeffe. The first painting by an African-American painter to be acquired by the White House—*Sand Dunes at Sunset, Atlantic City* by Henry Ossawa Tanner—hangs here, too. Rare and wonderful objects are on display in the Green Room. A silverplated coffee urn that President John Adams called one of his "most prized possessions" stands on a sofa table.

The GREEN Room

FACES &
VOICES *Nancy Clarke, Chief Floral Designer*

When White House guests admire the flower arrangements that grace every room, they are looking at the work of Nancy Clarke and her staff. Ms. Clarke has worked as the official White House florist since 1981, and was a volunteer here before that.

"I have worked for President Carter, President Reagan, President Bush, President Clinton, and now President George W. Bush," she says. Ms. Clarke and her staff of three begin their day early, around 6:30 A.M. "I come in and walk through the entire house and look at all the flowers that the people on tours will see," she says. "I check everything out. If they're fine we just water them. If they need to be changed, we do that. Fresh flowers arrive around ten o'clock, and four of us get to work on new arrangements."

The florists have four areas to cover: the rooms on the State Floor; the Family Residence on the second floor; the West Wing, including the Oval Office; and arrangements for special events such as State Dinners and wreath-laying ceremonies for presidential gravesites.

"We do traditional arrangements for the State Floor," Ms. Clarke says. "It's a very traditional house. A bowl of flowers for the Red Room should look like it belongs in the Red Room, not in an art gallery. For the parlors we coordinate with the colors of each room. In the Green Room, for example, we work with the colors in the carpet and the draperies."

To prepare for her position, Ms. Clarke studied floral design and has taken many art classes. She works closely with the first lady to make sure her work fits the family's preferences. "President and Mrs. Bush really like white roses," she says.

For a State Dinner, Ms. Clarke meets with the first lady to talk about the look she wants to have for the event. "Then we select a tablecloth and tableware. We'll put together a sample place setting, put the flowers and everything together to make sure it's exactly what she wants. We make the flower arrangements either low so guests can see over them, or very high so they can see under them."

Ms. Clarke and her staff also make flower arrangements for Camp David, the presidential retreat in the mountains of Maryland. "We are the president's florist. If he needs something up at Camp David, we do it and send it along. If he needs something at the ranch in Texas, we send it along there."

Yellow rose of Texas. Nancy Clarke arranges roses, lilies, and spider chrysanthemums in the Diplomatic Reception Room.

Changing décor. The Blue Room has been redecorated many times. In President Grover Cleveland's day, it featured velvet couches. Today, furniture ordered by President James Monroe in 1817 has been put back in the room.

The BLUE Room

The oval Blue Room is the centerpiece of the State Floor at the White House. It has been used as the major White House reception room since 1800. Just about every president has shaken hands with visitors here—and many presidents and first ladies have turned their hands to redecorating the room.

The Blue Room overlooks the South Lawn and the Ellipse. Today it is furnished with a set of French Empire furniture bought by President James Monroe when he refurnished the White House after it was burned during the War of 1812. The blue silk upholstery of the elegant chairs and sofas are patterned with many motifs, including eagles and wreaths.

The room was refurbished with new wallpaper, fabrics, and carpet in 1995 during the Clinton administration, the most recent of many transformations. In 1837, President Martin Van Buren redecorated the room, using blue for the first time. In 1860, President James Buchanan sold the French Empire furniture and replaced it with heavier Victorian pieces. The Blue Room was very blue indeed from 1902 through 1962, with wall coverings and draperies of dark blue. In 1962, Mrs. Kennedy redecorated the room, covering the walls with lighter, cream striped silk. Over time, seven of the original chairs purchased by President Monroe were acquired and put back in the room; an original sofa joined them in 1979. Now, the furniture here is the oldest original furniture in the White House collection.

President and Mrs. Abraham Lincoln received members of Congress, diplomats, and other guests in the Blue Room on the historic day in 1863 when the president signed the Emancipation Proclamation.

Grover Cleveland, the only president to marry in the White House, wed Frances Folsom in the Blue Room in 1886.

The RED Room

When Dolley Madison held her Wednesday-evening parties, this parlor was decorated in yellows, not reds. The popular hostess kept a piano and guitar in the room. The elegant, comfortable Red Room has been used by most presidents and first ladies as a sitting room, although some small dinner parties have taken place here. During the nineteenth century, it made a cozy music room for family gatherings. For some years, the famous Gilbert Stuart portrait of George Washington hung here, and the room was called the Washington Parlor. First ladies' portraits filled the walls until First Lady Edith Roosevelt moved them downstairs in 1902. Redecorated in 1962, 1970, and 2000, the Red Room contains American Empire furniture similar to the French Empire pieces in the Blue Room. As the name suggests, this furniture was made in the United States.

Red all over. The Red Room has often been used as a sitting room. Gilded dolphins decorate the feet of the 19th-century sofa.

Portrait of Dolley Madison, by Gilbert Stuart, 1804

The STATE Dining Room

It is hard to imagine, but this elegant formal dining room was once decorated with stuffed animal heads. President Theodore Roosevelt enlarged and decorated the room in 1902 to accommodate big dinner parties. He also displayed a huge moose head over the mantel! At the end of his term, the president had lions' heads on the marble mantelpiece recarved into bison. He thought the American animal was more appropriate for the President's House. The stuffed animal heads were banished during the Warren Harding administration.

As it did in the early 1800s, a gilded and mirrored centerpiece called a plateau, which stretches more than 14 feet long, decorates the table. Three gilded bronze baskets sit on the plateau. Purchased from France by James Monroe in 1817, this treasure has been used by many presidents and continues to impress those who see it.

Gilded ornaments. This ornate gilded and mirrored table decoration, known as a plateau, is still used for special occasions.

Treasure chests. The White House silver was stored in special trunks until a pantry was built to hold it in the early 20th century.

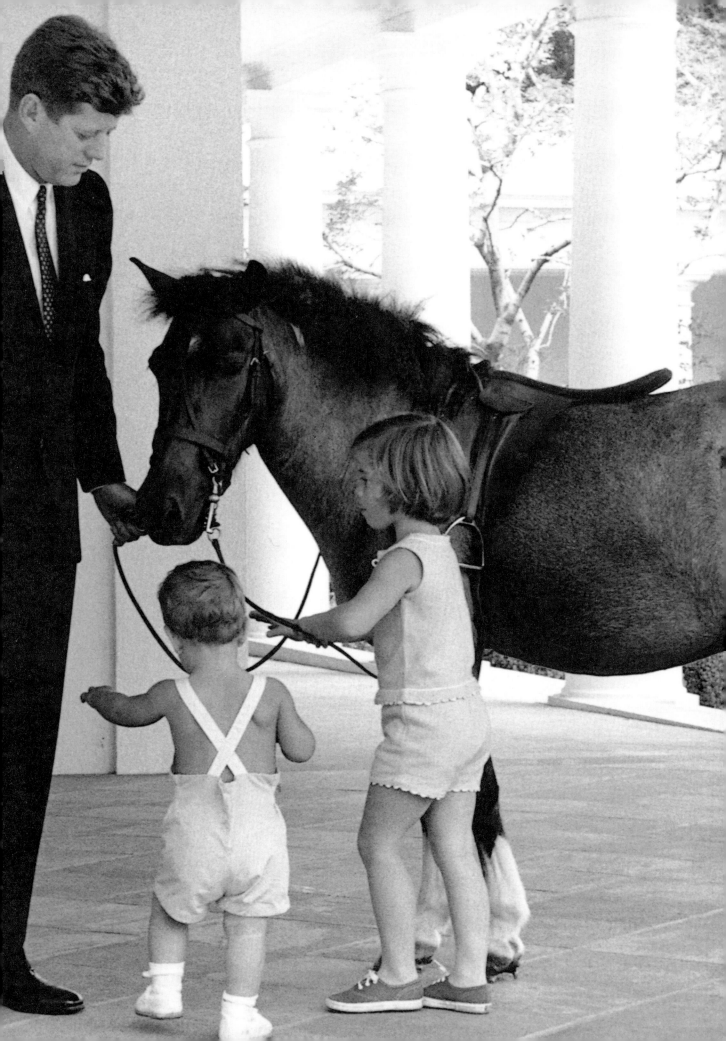

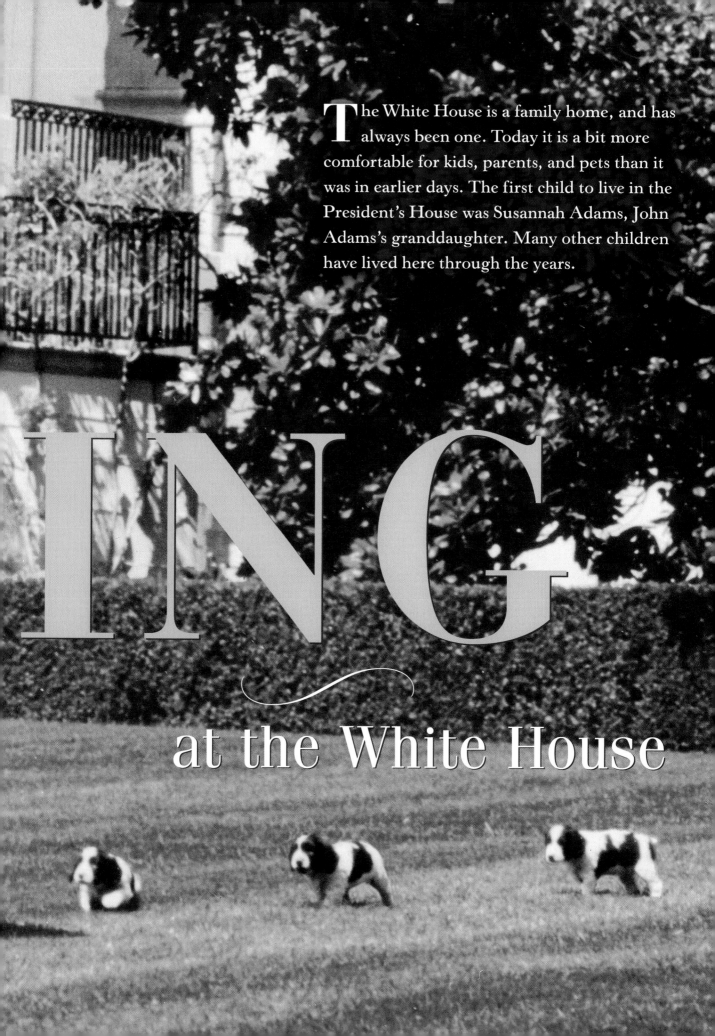

The White House is a family home, and has always been one. Today it is a bit more comfortable for kids, parents, and pets than it was in earlier days. The first child to live in the President's House was Susannah Adams, John Adams's granddaughter. Many other children have lived here through the years.

ING

at the White House

Snowball fight! President Franklin D. Roosevelt's grandchildren spent a lot of time at the White House. Here, they enjoy a winter snowfall.

Before the West Wing was built in 1902, first families, office workers, and crowds of visitors doing business with the president all used space on the second floor of the White House. The family quarters could be crowded, too. When Theodore Roosevelt's large family moved in, there were only eight rooms to accommodate all of them—and their many pets. The rest of the upstairs rooms were used as offices.

The White House is an impressive place, but kids will be kids, whether they live in an apartment house, a suburban house, or the White House. There are plenty of stories about first kids' mischief—many of them involving Theodore Roosevelt's family of six. Quentin Roosevelt, one of his sons, once put a pony in the White House elevator and took the animal upstairs. He was just trying to cheer up his brother Archie, who was sick. Quentin and his friends also threw spitballs at a portrait of President Andrew Jackson. Caroline Kennedy once brought her muddy-hooved pony Macaroni into her father's office.

White House kids find special ways to make the White House seem like a regular home. Tad Lincoln, President Abraham Lincoln's youngest son, made some extra money selling lemonade to the people who visited the White House. Amy Carter, with the help of the White House grounds superintendent, built a tree house on the South Lawn. Her father, President Jimmy Carter, drew the plans for the tree house himself. It was designed so that no nails would injure the tree's bark.

Closed gatefold: New additions. President George Bush, Millie, and her puppies on the South Lawn.

Open gatefold: President meets pony. Caroline and John Jr. visit their father, President John F. Kennedy, outside the Oval Office. They are joined by Macaroni, the children's pony.

The FAMILY Quarters

Family time. President Lyndon Johnson takes some time out from leading the country to play with his grandson.

Homework calls. Susan Ford works on her school assignments in her bedroom in the family quarters.

The second and third floors of the White House are off-limits to the public. There are fifteen family and guest bedrooms and fifteen bathrooms. Some of the rooms, such as the Lincoln Bedroom, which is filled with furniture, documents, and objects that are associated with the sixteenth president, are like museums. But guests do stay in them. Others are just ordinary rooms like yours at home—except that the president and his family happen to live in them!

There is a kitchen and dining room where the first family can enjoy meals in private. There is a formal sitting room called the Yellow Oval Room. There the president and first lady can relax on their own or meet with family, friends, or very special guests.

A sunny solarium tops the house, with a spectacular view of the Ellipse, the Washington Monument, and the Jefferson Memorial.

When they move in, members of the first family can choose furnishings from a government storage facility filled with beds, tables, and dressers. Many of these pieces are historic objects. The Office of the Curator prepares loose-leaf notebooks with photographs of available items. Amy Carter chose a suite of child-size Victorian furniture for her room. Families also bring personal items and family photographs to make the White House feel familiar, of course. Like you, young people in the White House can invite friends over to visit or for sleepovers.

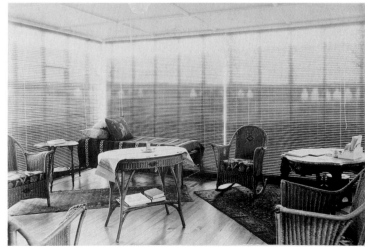

Time to relax. Ronald and Nancy Reagan enjoy a simple supper in the family quarters (top). Before air conditioning, the first family could retreat to a porch atop the White House to catch a breeze (above).

Rebecca the raccoon. First Lady Grace Coolidge cuddles her unusual pet.

A Place for PETS

Pets have lightened the atmosphere of the most important home in the country since the beginning. Early presidents all had horses and carriages for transportation, of course, and the President's House sometimes had its own milk cows and even sheep. Inside, domestic pets offered laughter and relaxation to the president and his family. Some had unusual animals. Thomas Jefferson had a pet mockingbird named Dick, who would hop up the stairs beside him when the president retired for the evening. Theodore Roosevelt Jr. had a pet macaw named Eli Yale. Other Roosevelt pets included raccoons, snakes, and badgers—and some plain old dogs. Grace Coolidge had a pet raccoon named Rebecca.

First pony. A White House policeman holds Algonquin, as Quentin Roosevelt gets ready to ride.

Presidential flock. During President Woodrow Wilson's administration, hungry sheep helped keep the White House lawns tidy and saved manpower.

Roll over! Fala, FDR's Scottish terrier, went everywhere with the president.

Beloved dogs and cats can help relieve some of the stress and isolation of living in the White House. President Warren G. Harding and his wife, Florence, were devoted to their Airedale, Laddie Boy, who was trained to retrieve tennis balls when the president missed a shot. President Herbert Hoover had several dogs who would join him on the lawn when he exercised. President Franklin D. Roosevelt never went anywhere without his Scottie, Fala. A biography of Fala was published in 1942; nearly fifty years later President George Bush's dog Millie published her autobiography about life in the White House (with some writing help from First Lady Barbara Bush). Today, Millie's daughter Spot accompanies President George W. Bush to the office. Spot was born in the White House in 1989 and is the first second-generation presidential pet. The Bushes' younger dog, a Scottie named Barney, hangs out elsewhere in the White House. Both dogs love it when President Bush relaxes by hitting old tennis balls for them to retrieve on the South Lawn.

Socks the cat. Chelsea Clinton brought her beloved pet to the White House from Arkansas when her father, Bill Clinton, became president.

A dog's life. President Warren G. Harding plays with Laddie Boy (above). The Airedale "hosted" the Easter Egg Roll one year when Harding was out of town. Millie, President George Bush's English springer spaniel, helps out at the White House switchboard (left).

FACES & VOICES
Dale Haney, Horticulturist and Pet Handler

Dale Haney, horticulturist, oversees the gardens around the White House. Mr. Haney works for the National Park Service, which is responsible for the outdoor areas of the mansion. But he also has another, very special job: He takes care of the president's dogs. Mr. Haney came to work at the White House as a gardener in 1973, when President Nixon was in the White House. He quickly got involved with all types of presidential pets.

"The Fords had golden retrievers," he recalls. "The Carters had a Siamese cat, but she stayed inside." These days, Haney spends a lot of time with President Bush's dogs. "In the mornings, the president brings the dogs down. I take Barney, and he walks with me while I walk the driveway to see if any branches came down in the night and things like that, and try to figure out what the

plans are going to be for the day. Spot goes to work with the president. She stays with him for an hour or an hour and a half. Then when Spot comes out of the Oval Office, the dogs get fed and Barney will go and stay with Mrs. Bush for awhile."

Mr. Haney says he gets pretty attached to his presidential pet pals. He's especially fond of Spot and Barney. "I love animals, and these two are great," he says. "I'll be out here on the grounds working in the flower beds, and they'll hang around with me. Spot will drop a ball in the pool and wait for it to get to a certain spot, and then she'll jump in after it. I knew Spot as a puppy," he says, petting her. "She came back here for her retirement."

Mr. Haney doesn't have a dog of his own at the moment, although for many years he had a golden retriever given to him by President Gerald Ford.

Playtime. Barney and Spot get ready to chase a tennis ball that Dale Haney will hit for them on the South Lawn.

Off to school. In the 1870s, President Ulysses S. Grant's children were taken to class in a horse-drawn carriage.

If you lived here
Going
OUT

Arriving home. President George W. Bush salutes a military aide as he disembarks from Marine One, the presidential helicopter.

The president and his family do not spend every moment in the White House, of course. But when they do go out, they do not do their own driving. When the president goes out, a motorcade—a line of cars and motorcycles— goes with him. The parade of vehicles begins with a police escort, then a Secret Service car, and then two nearly identical presidential limousines. The president rides in one of them. The other one is a decoy. Other cars carry staff, the president's doctor, and an aide who carries communications equipment that allows the president to instantly reach the Pentagon and the White House in a crisis. Another aide carries a briefcase containing emergency codes. (Staffers call this briefcase "the football.") More vans loaded with photographers and reporters follow along. An ambulance brings up the rear. When he is at his ranch in Texas, President George W. Bush trades the presidential limo for a sport utility vehicle with the Presidential Seal on the door.

Executive transportation. Flags flutter from the president's car as Air Force One, the presidential jet, is readied for takeoff. This "flying White House" takes the president all over the world.

Leaving the White House is not such a big deal for members of the family, but they are escorted by Secret Service officers wherever they go—even on dates and shopping trips. Families who live in the White House have wonderful opportunities to meet famous people, be at the center of power, and live in a historic home. But they give up a lot of privacy, too.

We like Ike. Outgoing President Harry S. Truman shares a ride with President-elect Dwight D. Eisenhower on Inauguration Day in 1953.

If you lived here
Staying IN

It may be more difficult to go out when you live at 1600 Pennsylvania Avenue—but it's pretty easy to stay in! Just about any kind of entertainment you can think of is available. There is a single-lane bowling alley that was put in by President Richard Nixon. There is a private movie theater with extra-comfortable seats. The first family can order any movie they want and watch it in comfort and safety. The kitchen staff will happily make popcorn or other snacks. On the South Lawn there is an outdoor swimming pool, a basketball court, a putting green, a tennis court, a horseshoe pit, and a jogging track.

Burgers, anyone? President Dwight D. Eisenhower cooks out on the terrace atop the White House (above).

Car wash. Susan Ford rinses off her car in the service area near the tradesmen's entrance to the White House (right).

First snowman. President Ronald Reagan and his son, Michael, help the president's grandchildren build a snowman in the Rose Garden (above).

Pass the popcorn. George and Barbara Bush relax in the White House movie theater with their family and friends. A grandson snuggles up to the first lady (left).

When President and Mrs. John F. Kennedy lived in the White House, they worried about protecting their children's privacy. Mrs. Kennedy created a White House school for Caroline. It was located in the solarium on the top floor of the house. Mrs. Kennedy often helped teach the children there. Caroline and John Jr. also had a playground on the grounds, complete with a trampoline.

Living in the White House can be lots of fun! It also puts families right in the center of history. Maybe you will live in the White House someday. If you do, like the other people who have called this house their home, you will honor its past—and make your own history there.

FACES & VOICES

Nancy Theis, Director of Presidential Student Correspondence

If numbers mean anything, America's youth feel close to the first family. Every day, thousands of letters pour into the White House from young people across the country. Some correspondents send photos or drawings. Some send in hand-made presents to the first family. Others send videos of school plays, show-and-tell time, or scouting events.

Of course, the president cannot answer *all* his mail personally. He just doesn't have the time! But he is interested in what students have to say and he wants very much to keep in touch with them. The Office of Presidential Student Correspondence, under the direction of Nancy Theis, helps out. Volunteers and staff members make sure that each letter is answered. Children who write in will often receive photos of the president, first lady, or their pets.

Before joining President Bush's staff, Ms. Theis handled similar responsibilities during the eight years of the Reagan administration and the four years of the first Bush administration. She recalls that President Reagan loved to read children's mail. "We would send him a packet each week that he would often take to Camp David in Maryland or out to his ranch in California," she says. "When he returned he would bring back with him lengthy handwritten letters to

forward to the girls and boys who wrote to him. President George Bush was great at sending personal notes. He often responded to students with short, snappy handwritten replies of his own."

Ms. Theis and her staff work in an office near the White House where the mail from young people of all ages ends up. After it is answered, it is sent to the National Archives and in the future will be forwarded to George W. Bush's presidential library.

One letter particularly stands out in Ms. Theis's memory. The envelope was addressed to: "President George W. Bush, Vice President Richard Cheney, Secretary of State Colin Powell, Secretary of Defense Donald Rumsfeld—or anyone else who will listen!"

"Each letter to the president receives a response so that young Americans will know that someone *is* listening!" she says.

Mail call. Nancy Theis and her colleagues respond to thousands of letters and artworks that children send to the first family.

Epilogue:
A WHITE HOUSE
Album

George and Martha Washington, 1789–1797

The first president and his wife never lived in the White House. But Washington, a surveyor and builder who loved houses, chose the site for the mansion, selected the architect, and saw building begin before he left office.

John and Abigail Adams, 1797–1801

John Adams moved into the White House while it was still incomplete. His wife, Abigail, joined him and they lived there for only a few months. Abigail Adams did not enjoy living in the unfinished building—although she loved the sweeping view of the Potomac River from its windows.

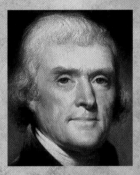

Thomas Jefferson, 1801–1809

Thomas Jefferson began the tradition of entertaining on the South Lawn of the President's House, holding lively Fourth of July celebrations there. He opened the doors of the house so that citizens could see the president's home. When Lewis and Clark sent back animal and plant specimens from their western expedition, Jefferson displayed them in the White House and invited the public to see them. Jefferson's married daughter Martha Randolph sometimes served as hostess because his wife had died before he became president. Martha had a baby during her father's term—the first child born in the President's House.

James and Dolley Madison, 1809–1817

During their early days in the mansion, the Madisons gave brilliant parties in the beautifully decorated rooms. But they were driven from the house by British troops during the War of 1812. Fire gutted the house; only scorched walls remained standing.

President Madison insisted that the President's House be rebuilt according to the original plans approved by George Washington. He even hired the original architect, James Hoban, to do the job.

James and Elizabeth Monroe, 1817–1825

James and Elizabeth Monroe had lived in Paris when he was the ambassador to France. They decorated parts of the rebuilt mansion in elegant French style and bought many important pieces of furniture and decorative objects that are still in the White House. President Monroe also added the curving South Portico in 1824.

Andrew Jackson, 1829–1837

A famous general in the War of 1812, Andrew Jackson was a man of the people who came from an ordinary background and invited all classes of people to the White House. Yet the house was also elegantly decorated, especially the East Room. He would change the presidency by assuming more executive power. He asserted federal over state rights and insisted that the president could appoint his own Cabinet. During his tenure in the White House, Jackson completed the North Portico, creating a formal entrance that is still in use.

which previously had been heated only by fireplaces. Because his wife, Hannah, died before he was elected president, his daughter-in-law Angelica Singleton Van Buren, a cousin of Dolley Madison, served as his hostess.

William Henry and Anna Harrison, 1841

President Harrison lived in the White House only thirty days. He caught pneumonia and died on April 4, 1841— exactly one month after taking the oath of office. He was the first president to die in office and to lie in state in the White House. His wife, Anna, never had a chance to leave their farm in Ohio and come to the White House to join him.

John Quincy and Louisa Catherine Adams, 1825–1829

John Quincy Adams enjoyed gardening and put much energy into planting the White House grounds. He created a museum of American plants there, especially trees. President Adams enjoyed walking downhill to the Potomac River for a swim.

Martin Van Buren, 1837–1841

During the first year of his presidency, President Van Buren redecorated the oval reception room at the center of the presidential mansion in shades of blue, beginning the tradition of the Blue Room, which continues today. Van Buren also added a hot-air heating system to the building,

John, Letitia (died 1842), and Julia Tyler, 1841–1845

President Tyler's first wife joined him at the White House, but her poor health prevented her from entertaining. Their daughter-in-law Priscilla Cooper served as hostess. After Letitia Tyler died, President Tyler remarried—the first president to marry while in office. His new wife, Julia, loved to entertain and gave dazzling parties.

Zachary and Margaret Taylor, 1849–1850

Called "Old Rough and Ready," this hero of the Mexican War brought his horse "Old Whitey" to the White House. The animal became one of the first celebrity pets. People even plucked hairs from its tail to keep as souvenirs. Taylor died in office in 1850.

Franklin and Jane Pierce, 1853–1857

President Pierce employed a full-time bodyguard whose only job was to protect the president—a preview of today's Secret Service. Mrs. Pierce, in mourning for her ten-year-old son Benny, who had been killed in a train accident before the family moved to Washington, rarely hosted parties in the Executive Mansion. President Pierce introduced some comforts to the White House: He had hot and cold running water piped into the upstairs bathroom.

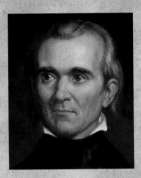

James K. and Sarah Polk, 1845–1849

President Polk appointed a steward to meet people at the White House door and usher them to appointments. This position, called the usher, endures today. The Polks brought gas lighting to the White House, adapting the East Room chandeliers to the new technology. Polk added a statue of Thomas Jefferson to the North Lawn. Both presidents expanded the nation westward.

Millard and Abigail Fillmore, 1850–1853

Millard and Abigail Fillmore established the first library in the White House. Mrs. Fillmore had been a teacher. Shocked to find no books in the house, Mrs. Fillmore asked Congress for money to establish a permanent collection, then she personally selected the books. The Fillmores had a music room and three pianos in their White House. President Fillmore, trained as a lawyer, was known for hard work; he kept his office in the mansion open seven days a week.

James Buchanan, 1857–1861

President Buchanan, the only president who never married, brought his niece Harriet Lane, known as "Hal," to serve as hostess in the White House. He had raised her from the age of eleven, when she was orphaned. Hal was popular and gave many gala parties. People called her "The Democratic Queen." Buchanan filled his house staff with British servants.

Abraham and Mary Lincoln, 1861–1865

The Civil War broke out only a few weeks after Abraham and Mary Lincoln and their three sons moved into the White House. The South Lawn was used as a military parade ground. In spite of the war, Mrs. Lincoln continued to give parties and spent large sums of money redecorating the house, which made her unpopular in the press. In 1862, the Lincolns' son Willie died in the White House. His funeral was held in the East Room. Three years later, Lincoln was assassinated and lay in state in the same room.

Andrew and Eliza Johnson, 1865–1869

With the Civil War over, Andrew Johnson's term of office saw extensive renovations of the White House. The president's daughter Martha Patterson, who served as his hostess because her mother was ill, oversaw the redecoration. President Johnson had a group

of presidential portraits hung in the house. A tradition of displaying presidential portraits continues today.

Ulysses S. and Julia Grant, 1869–1877

The Grants and their four children lived in the White House for eight years. The Civil War hero and his wife were popular, and people appreciated the balls, receptions, and dinners that they gave. Their daughter Nellie was married in the White House. President Grant added a billiard room and had the East Room redone, adding beams and gilding. Julia Grant enjoyed living in the Executive Mansion. "I love the dear old house," she wrote.

Rutherford B. and Lucy Hayes, 1877–1881

President Hayes installed a telephone in the White House on a trial basis. There were few people to call in those days because so few people had the devices. But phones have been in the White House ever since —now 5,000 calls are received a day. The Hayes's children, who went to school in an upstairs corridor, installed a dollhouse there. During this term, the South Lawn of the White House was enclosed in a high fence. The Easter Egg Roll moved there from the Capitol lawn in 1879.

James R. and Lucretia Garfield, 1881

President Garfield served as president for only 121 days before he was shot by a man who had been refused a job. He lingered for two months, his wife nursing him, but he died in September 1881. As President Garfield lay dying in the steamy, hot Washington summer, engineers rigged up a

system of tubes and fans that wafted cool air from ice in the White House basement to cool him. This system demonstrated the basic principles of air-conditioning.

Chester A. Arthur, 1881–1885

Chester A. Arthur did not like the White House, finding it old-fashioned and inconvenient. He hired the famous designer Louis Comfort Tiffany to redecorate. Tiffany installed a long, red-white-and-blue stained-glass screen in the Entrance Hall. President Arthur's extensive renovations cost $110,000— a great deal of money in the 1880s. It was the largest sum spent on the White House since it was rebuilt after the 1814 fire. A widower, he asked his sister, Mary Arthur McElroy, to serve as his official hostess.

Grover and Frances Cleveland, 1885–1889

The only first couple to be married in the White House, the Clevelands had a small candlelit ceremony in the Blue Room. At twenty-one, Mrs. Cleveland was the youngest first lady ever. She was very popular and many stories appeared in the newspapers about her. When the Clevelands moved out of the White House after his defeat in the election, she told the staff she would be back. She was right. Cleveland was reelected four years later.

Benjamin and Caroline Harrison, 1889–1893

President and Mrs. Harrison invited their adult children and their grandchildren to live with them in the White House. Mrs. Harrison drew up plans to enlarge the White House to accommodate her extended family, but Congress would not allocate the money. However,

the Harrisons did modernize: They had electricity installed. Mrs. Harrison enjoyed being first lady, but she became ill with tuberculosis and died in the White House in 1892, at the age of sixty.

Grover and Frances Cleveland, 1893–1897

When they moved back into the White House for a second administration, the Clevelands had all the state rooms repainted and all the rooms in the private quarters refreshed. During this term, the president and first lady had a daughter, Esther, the first baby born to a president and first lady in the White House. (Another child, Esther's older sister Ruth had a candy bar named after her—the Baby Ruth.)

William and Ida McKinley, 1897–1901

President McKinley was in the White House for the one-hundredth anniversary of the day when John Adams moved into the President's House. He and his wife, Ida, who was in frail health, lived quietly there. Although plans for large additions were discussed, they were not built. The McKinleys did renovate the Blue Room in the colonial style. President McKinley was assassinated in 1901. Like Lincoln's, his body lay in state in the East Room.

Theodore and Edith Roosevelt, 1901–1909

When the boisterous "Teddy" Roosevelt and his young family of six children moved into the White House, the building was transformed by active children and many pets. The noise would not stop for eight years! In 1902, President Roosevelt also transformed it with a major renovation, enlarging the State Dining Room and adding the East Wing and the Executive Office Building next to the mansion—later called the "West Wing."

William Howard and Helen Taft, 1909–1913

President Taft made a significant addition to the White House: He built the original Oval Office. Oval in shape to echo the curved rooms in the center of the White House, the office was on the south side of the Executive Office Building. Although it was relocated later, an Oval Office has functioned as the president's workplace from that time to the present. Mrs. Taft made a significant contribution, too—but to the city of Washington, not the White House. She arranged for the planting of 3,000 cherry trees given to the United States as a gift from Japan. These are the originals of Washington, D.C.'s famous cherry blossoms.

Woodrow, Ellen (died 1914), and Edith Wilson, 1913–1921

The beginning of Woodrow Wilson's presidency was shadowed not only by World War I but also by the death of his wife Ellen, who had loved gardens and extensively changed those at the White House. She established the first rose garden on the west side of the mansion and created the East Garden. Wilson remarried in 1915. When he became very ill at the end of his term, his second wife, Edith, took over some of his work.

Warren G. and Florence Harding, 1921–1923

During President Harding's administration, many celebrations and traditions that had been suspended during World War I were revived. New Year's Day receptions came back; Easter Egg Rolls returned to the South Lawn. The Hardings' handsome dog Laddie Boy made headlines. But in 1923, Harding died suddenly while on a trip to California,

another president to lie in state in the East Room before his funeral.

Calvin and Grace Coolidge, 1923–1929

During the Coolidge administration, engineers determined that the upper stories of the White House were in bad shape. Extensive repairs included the addition of a third story of rooms where the White House attic had been. A solarium, or sunroom, was also added. This sunny, private room with a breathtaking view of the Washington Monument and the Mall has remained a favorite of presidential families ever since. The room, originally called a "sky parlor," was Mrs. Coolidge's idea.

Herbert and Lou Hoover, 1929–1933

The beginning of the Hoover administration was efficient and cheerful, but the stock market crash of 1929 and the economic depression that followed cast gloom over the White House. Then, in the Christmas season of 1929, a fire gutted the Executive Office Building, but it was soon rebuilt. Because of the Hoovers' interest in history, the White House furnishings and decorations began to be catalogued and studied as important parts of the story of our nation and the President's House.

Franklin D. and Eleanor Roosevelt, 1933–1945

Franklin and Eleanor Roosevelt lived in the White House longer than any other first family. An activist first lady who wrote and served as her husband's eyes and ears as she traveled, Mrs. Roosevelt had little interest in furniture and decoration, although she did oversee restoration of the Red Room. Much changed in the house during the twelve years the Roosevelts lived there. An indoor swimming pool was added so that the president, crippled by polio, could exercise. The West Wing was enlarged and rebuilt, with the Oval Office moving to its present location overlooking the Rose Garden. The White House ground floor was overhauled, and spaces were designed for a new Library and other rooms off the vaulted hallway; kitchens were remodeled. During World War II, a movie theater was built behind the East Colonnade and an air-raid shelter was created in an expanded East Wing. Security increased as the president directed the war effort. In 1945, exhausted and ill, Roosevelt died in Georgia. His body was returned to Washington by train. Five days later, Mrs. Roosevelt moved out of the home she had lived in for twelve years.

Harry S. and Bess Truman, 1945–1953

The largest renovation of the White House took place during the Truman administration. Discovering that floors were in danger of falling in, the Trumans moved out and the house was gutted. After a concrete and steel structure was put up inside, all the rooms were reassembled. Subbasements were dug and new rooms added. The process took several years. In 1952, the president and first lady moved back across the street from Blair House, where they had been living. President Truman went on national television to give the American people a tour of their renovated White House.

Dwight D. and Mamie Eisenhower, 1953–1961

Seven years after World War II, the great general Dwight D. Eisenhower moved into the White House as president. He and his wife, Mamie, entertained a stream of heads of state from around the world. Mrs. Eisenhower became interested in using antiques in the White House, sponsoring the redecoration of the Diplomatic Reception Room as a Federal-period parlor. The Eisenhowers lived comfortably in the rebuilt White House for eight years.

John F. and Jacqueline Kennedy, 1961–1963

The Kennedys used the White House to host important cultural events and showcase American artists. John F. Kennedy launched America's race to the moon here, and brought the nation through the Cuban Missile Crisis, when nuclear war threatened. Only thirty-two when she became first lady, Jacqueline Kennedy

brought her background in art, history, and culture to bear on the White House. She helped found the White House Historical Association and worked to have museum-quality objects and artwork acquired for the White House. She restored the State Floor rooms and guided America through them on television.

Lyndon and Lady Bird Johnson, 1963–1969

President and Mrs. Lyndon Johnson completed the Kennedy plans for restoring the State Rooms. Lady Bird Johnson, who was very interested in nature and wildflowers, launched a successful campaign to beautify the American landscape. She commissioned new White House china that featured the American eagle in the center with a border of wildflowers. During the Johnson administration, the White House was shown off to advantage at the celebration of the marriage of one of his daughters. Entertaining became less formal than in the

Kennedy era—Texas-style barbecues were thrown on the South Lawn. The Johnsons donated the Children's Garden, which is still enjoyed today.

Gerald and Betty Ford, 1974–1977

During Gerald and Betty Ford's time in the White House, their teenage daughter Susan reminded people that the White House was a family home. Susan washed her car by the tradesmen's entrance and hosted her senior prom in the East Room. President Ford built an outdoor pool to get his favorite kind of exercise. The White House was a place for active family life. The Fords also continued the tradition of acquiring objects for the White House's permanent collection, notably important American paintings.

Richard M. and Patricia Nixon, 1969–1974

Richard and Patricia Nixon brought their love for American history to their relationship with the White House. Mrs. Nixon oversaw a restoration project. With the guidance of the White House curator, many fine antiques with White House associations were acquired, especially furniture made before 1840. A number of early furnishings were brought to the President's House, and the rooms in the public areas of the house reflected the mansion's early history. Nixon was successful in many diplomatic endeavors, including opening relations with China, but after the Watergate scandal, he resigned his office.

Jimmy and Rosalynn Carter, 1977–1981

When the Carters moved into the White House, their daughter Amy was the youngest presidential child to live there since the Kennedy administration. The Carters' informal style was signaled when they walked hand in hand down Pennsylvania Avenue from the swearing in at the Capitol. This style continued in their approach to living at the White House. The Marine Band stopped playing "Hail to the Chief" when the president appeared at an event. Amy attended public school. The president was even seen carrying his own suitcase when he traveled.

Ronald and Nancy Reagan, 1981–1989

Ronald and Nancy Reagan brought a more formal style back to the White House. Their first project was to redecorate the family quarters, raising private funds to do so. Nancy Reagan also acquired new White House china for State Dinners. During their eight years in the White House, the Reagans brought Hollywood glamour to their entertaining. Ronald Reagan survived an assassination attempt early in his presidency and went on to serve two terms.

George and Barbara Bush, 1989–1993

George and Barbara Bush's White House style was relaxed and informal, filled with grandchildren and dogs. One dog, Millie, even wrote her autobiography—with Mrs. Bush's help. Mrs. Bush used the visibility of her White House position to encourage literacy. President Bush led the nation during the Gulf War. The relaxed, family-oriented Bush White House style seemed to relieve some of the pressure of this international conflict.

Bill Clinton and Hillary Rodham Clinton, 1993–2001

The Clintons were deeply involved in planning for and observing the 200th anniversary of the White House and the millennium celebration in 2000. New china was commissioned for the White House collection. Meanwhile, daughter Chelsea grew up, graduated from high school, and went off to college. The Clintons fiercely protected her privacy, allowing her to have as normal a life as possible when you live in the White House. During his administration, Clinton survived impeachment hearings in Congress that would have removed him from office. He also oversaw an economic boom in America. During the Clinton presidency, the first lady assumed a new role, taking on policy responsibilities and public duties—a role she plays formally today as a U.S. senator from New York State.

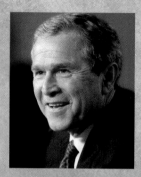

George W. and Laura Bush, 2001–

Only months after President and Mrs. George W. Bush moved into the White House, the September 11 attacks on New York and Washington changed the way business is done at the White House. Security increased and entertaining was scaled back for a nation at war. However, the Bushes' commitment to keeping the White House available to the American people meant tours for school and veteran groups have started again. The Easter Egg Roll, garden tours, and the Fourth of July are celebrated with joy and spirit. Mrs. Bush, at first inclined to stay out of the spotlight, has stepped forward to help console Americans and rally their spirits.

SELECTED BIBLIOGRAPHY

Hundreds of books have been written about the White House and the first families who have lived there. I consulted many books while writing this one. The list below represents the twenty books I found most useful. Among them, *The President's House*, a two-volume history by William Seale, was indispensable.

Aikman, Lonnelle. *The Living White House*, tenth edition. Washington, D.C.: White House Historical Association, 1996.

Bausum, Ann. *Our Country's Presidents*. Washington, D.C.: National Geographic Society, 2001.

Coulter, Laurie. *When John and Caroline Lived in the White House.* New York: Hyperion, 2000.

Debnam, Betty. *A Kid's Guide to the White House.* Washington, D.C.: White House Historical Association, 1997.

Feinberg, Barbara Silberdick. *The Changing White House.* New York: Children's Press, 2000.

Garrett, Wendell, ed. *Our Changing White House.* Boston: Northeastern University Press, 1995.

Freidel, Frank and Hugh Sidey. *The Presidents of the United States of America*, sixteenth edition. Washington, D.C.: White House Historical Association, 2001.

Freidel, Frank, and William Pencak, eds. *The White House: The First Two Hundred Years.* Boston: Northeastern University Press, 1994.

Karr, Kathleen. *It Happened in the White House.* New York: Scholastic Inc., 2000.

Kirk, Elise K. *Musical Highlights from the White House.* Malabar, Florida: Krieger Publishing Company, 1992.

Klapthor, Margaret Brown and Allida Black. *The First Ladies*, ninth edition. Washington, D.C.: White House Historical Association, 2001.

Kloss, William, Doreen Bolger, David Park Curry, John Wilmerding, Betty C. Monkman. *Art in the White House: A Nation's Pride.* Washington, D.C.: White House Historical Association, 1992.

Leiner, Katherine. *First Children: Growing up in the White House.* New York: William Morrow, 1996.

Monkman, Betty C. *The White House: Its Historic Furnishings and First Families.* Washington, D.C.: Abbeville Press and White House Historical Association, 2000.

Seale, William. *The President's House*, Vols. I and II. Washington, D.C.: White House Historical Association, 1986.

Seale, William. *The White House Garden.* Washington, D.C.: White House Historical Association, 1996.

Singleton, Esther. *The Story of the White House.* New York: The McClure Company, 1907.

Waters, Kate. *The Story of the White House.* New York: Scholastic Inc., 1999.

Whitcomb, John, and Claire Whitcomb. *Real Life at the White House.* New York: Routledge, 2000.

White House Historical Association. *The White House: An Historic Guide*, twenty-first edition. Washington, D.C.: White House Historical Association, 2001.

FOR MORE INFORMATION

The internet offers several resources for readers interested in up-to-the-minute information about the White House and the presidents and their families who have lived there. These are the most informative:

The White House Web site
www.whitehouse.gov
This official United States government site offers daily news, histories of the presidents and first ladies, contemporary photo essays, and much more—including a link to a site for kids. To access the kids' site directly, go to www.whitehouse.kids.gov

The White House Historical Association Web site
www.whitehousehistory.org
This site is the place to go for the history of the White House and its historic collection of objects. The WHHA also provides special areas on its site for teachers and for kids. You can purchase White House Christmas ornaments, books, and cards through this site, as well as subscribe to *White House History,* an illustrated magazine about the mansion.

The Presidential Library Page
www.archives.gov/presidential_libraries
There are twelve official libraries, which house important papers and other material about twentieth-century presidents and offer exhibits about their administrations. There are libraries for Bill Clinton, George Bush, Ronald Reagan, Jimmy Carter, Gerald R. Ford, Richard Nixon, Lyndon Johnson, John F. Kennedy, Dwight D. Eisenhower, Harry S. Truman, Franklin D. Roosevelt, and Herbert Hoover. To find out more about a president who interests you, go to the National Archives presidential libraries page and click on a name.

OTHER MEDIA

Echoes from the White House: A Celebration of the Bicentennial of America's Mansion
This Public Television video uses the actual words of presidents, first ladies, and other eyewitnesses to tell the story of the White House from 1800 to 2000.

Inside the White House
This National Geographic video takes the viewer on a behind-the-scenes tour, including a look at the private quarters.

Within These Walls: A Visit to the White House and *Upon These Grounds: Exploring the White House Garden*
These two White House Historical Association videos take the viewer on up-close tours.

The White House Is Our House
This White House Historical Association CD-ROM offers an interactive experience of the White House, its historic furnishings, and its grounds.

Dear Mr. President

Would you like to send a letter to the president or first lady? It is easy. Write your letter and mail it to:

The White House
1600 Pennsylvania Avenue N.W.
Washington, D.C. 20500

Children may also fax letters to 1-202-456-7705.

All letters are answered, but do not expect to hear back right away. The White House receives thousands of pieces of mail, and it can take time to sort through and answer them all.

Index